"*Charles Powell has been a strong presence in* [...] *provided security and protection to celebrities and has* [...] *needed it. I have watched his writing evolve for over a decade. This book is about an issue that haunts America and the world—a vitally important topic. The subject matter is nothing short of pure evil—and how do we defeat it.*"

—LUIS URREA, 2005 Pulitzer Prize finalist for nonfiction and member of the Latino Literature Hall of Fame

"*People are not stirred by sympathy but are moved by empathy. Charles Powell and Dillon Burroughs have given the world an empathetic, verbal photograph of the intolerable and unbelievable dimensions of human slavery in the twenty-first century. Not in My Town will shock you out of the complacency of your comfort zone as you read the pitiful plight of 30 million people on planet Earth and realize that America is one of the top three havens in the world for human trafficking. Charles Powell and Dillon Burroughs will make you feel a firestorm of mixed emotions and then it will make you mad; hopefully, mad enough to eliminate the problem!*"

—DR. RONALD W. CARPENTER, SR., presiding bishop, International Pentecostal Holiness Church

"*This book is a must-read. Even from a survivor's point this book is very bold and truth telling. It hits the soul of those who wish to speak and feel we have no words to express our pain and what we go through. Charles and Dillon did a brilliant job bringing about the situations of what these victims have gone through, that we didn't 'choose' this circumstance as a slave didn't choose to be chattel.*"

—CHONG N. KIM, trafficking survivor, author, and abolitionist

"*Charles Powell has focused his investigative skills on a scourge too few of us knew existed. The scope of modern-day slavery is mind-boggling, its stories heartbreaking—and there's a good chance its victims are right in your own backyard! If you don't believe me, open this book and let Charles and Dillon take you on a tour of the seamy side of America. You'll never be the same.*"

—NATE LARKIN, founder of the Samson Society and author of Samson and the Pirate Monks: Calling Men to Authentic Brotherhood

"*What a privilege to recommend the work of Dillon and Charles to you! Each of them has impacted our lives at Home of Hope-Texas as they combat this evil called modern-day slavery and human trafficking. It is a great honor to have this book and video effort dedicated to my late wife, Sandra Bass Palmer. Our prayer is that as these servants 'pour the water' of Not in My Town, 'He will cause it to become wine' in your heart!*"

—MARK PALMER, administrator, Bringing Hope, Inc., Home of Hope-Texas

"Not in My Town *is a book for these times. Over the past 20 years I have traveled the world seeing glimpses of the reality of slavery. In the past 3 years I have seen firsthand hundreds of people enslaved, beaten, and/or sold. I am an eyewitness to what this book is all about.* Not in My Town *is exposing the modern-day exploitation of human beings in sex slavery, domestic servitude, and all kinds of forced labor. I applaud Charles Powell and Dillon Burroughs for communicating facts and real-life dramas in this unfolding story of human suffering. Both of these men are men of integrity and they have a heart to set the captives free!"*

—BRUCE LADEBU, founder and president of Children's Rescue Initiative
(www.thechildrensrescue.org)

"Modern human trafficking is not the image of slavery that first comes to mind. It is a hidden, barely visible system. No Middle Passage nor slave markets nor Southern plantations. And it's about more than sex. We likely all benefit from it, from the harvesting of the food we eat to the making of the clothes we wear. Not in My Town *helps us develop eyes for seeing and hands for responding."*

—LYLE SMITH GRAYBEAL, coordinator, Renovaré USA*

"My friend Charles Powell is one of those rare individuals who cares more about about righting the wrongs of society than maintaining the religious status quo. I admire his courage. And I pray that his bold attempt to confront and expose the evil of sex trafficking in the United States will wake up a sleeping church and ignite a fire for justice in all of us."

—J. LEE GRADY, journalist, author of *The Holy Spirit Is Not for Sale*
and *10 Lies the Church Tells Women*

"Charles Powell and Dillon Burroughs invite you to join them, to enter the world of human trafficking and modern slavery. They reveal the realities we too often ignore. They expose how nearby the abuse occurs. And their stories and conversations welcome us to enter the group of people who will refuse to ignore this topic."

—CHRIS MAXWELL, author, pastor, speaker,
spiritual life director, Royston, Georgia

NOT IN MY

TOWN

New Hope® Publishers
P. O. Box 12065
Birmingham, AL 35202-2065
www.newhopepublishers.com
New Hope Publishers is a division of WMU®.

Library of Congress Cataloging-in-Publication Data
Burroughs, Dillon.
  Not in my town : exposing and ending human trafficking and modern-day slavery / Dillon Burroughs, Charles Powell.
     p. cm.
  Includes bibliographical references (p.   ).
  ISBN 978-1-59669-301-2 (pbk.)
    1. Human trafficking--United States. 2. Human trafficking--United States--Prevention. 3. Prostitution--United States. 4. Prostitution--United States--Prevention. I. Powell, Charles, 1962- II. Title.
  HQ314.B87 2011
  306.3'620973--dc22

                    2011008816

Interior design: Glynese Northam

ISBN-10: 1-59669-301-0
ISBN-13: 978-1-59669-301-2
N114136 • 0511 • 5M

NOT IN MY TOWN

EXPOSING & ENDING

HUMAN TRAFFICKING & MODERN-DAY SLAVERY

DILLON BURROUGHS
★★★★★★★★★★★★★★★AND★★★★★★★★★★★★★★★
CHARLES POWELL

NEW HOPE
PUBLISHERS

BIRMINGHAM, ALABAMA

DEDICATION

We dedicate this book to Sandra Bass Palmer (1955–2010),

the first woman we met who loved Jesus and freeing girls from slavery

with equal passion. Her impact continues despite her departure

from this world. Many will be changed as a result.

CONTENTS

FOREWORD

SLAVERY STILL EXISTS. Though illegal in most every country of the world, forms of slavery continue in nearly every country of the world, including the United States. The US State Department estimates approximately 15,000 to 18,000 men, women, and children are trafficked into our nation each year. Whether for labor in sweatshops, as domestic servants, in agricultural slavery, or through sexual exploitation, the scourge of human trafficking continues to impact communities throughout our nation.

On the positive side, there are a growing number of individuals and organizations responding to America's growing human trafficking epidemic. My friends Charles J. Powell and Dillon Burroughs are among them. Through their efforts with the Mercy Movement, they have documented the darkness of the problem and are working toward solutions relevant to everyday citizens who desire to change the situation.

First, in these pages you will discover a greater awareness of trafficking within America's borders. From Atlanta to Orlando to Las Vegas, each community expresses its own form of criminal activity. However, through the local efforts of inspired citizens, often those expressing their Christian faith in action, changes are taking place that serve as a model to the rest of us in combating this evil.

Second, you'll find specific ways to speak out and stand against trafficking worldwide by taking action here in the United States. Taking a stand here is, in fact, taking a stance in the global war against trafficking. Sometimes, a single letter to the right person or company can create change. At other times, evaluating the labor source of your favorite products will mark a small step in moving companies toward fair trade in all American products. In addition, something you learn in this book may lead to ways you can directly intervene to assist victims by reporting potential human trafficking crimes or assisting in aftercare efforts.

Regardless of the response appropriate to your own life, the most important message communicated by Powell and Burroughs is that ending human trafficking in your own community begins with you. Only through a major response from everyday citizens will the sources that fuel the demand for human trafficking in local communities receive the necessary attention to end them. I encourage you to read these words carefully, reflect on how to apply them in your area, and take a stand against human trafficking where you live. May we all one day be able to say on the issue of human trafficking, "Not in my town."

— US CONGRESSMAN PAUL C. BROUN, JR., MD,
10th Congressional District of Georgia

ACKNOWLEDGMENTS

EVERY BOOK IS a team effort. We wish we could include the names of everyone involved in the making of this project, but both space and security issues will not allow. We apologize in advance for anyone not mentioned specifically below.

From the start, New Hope publisher Andrea Mullins fully supported our efforts to involve the church in the modern abolitionist movement. Without her example and leadership, these pages would not exist.

Likewise, New Hope's staff provided an outstanding array of artists, editors, and sales professionals who guided our dream from our laptops to your hands. To Publisher Andrea Mullins, Marketing and Sales Manager Jonathan Howe, Managing Editor Joyce Dinkins, Copy Editor Kathryne Solomon, and the rest of the New Hope team, you have served well as both publishing professionals and fellow ministers of the hope available through Jesus Christ.

CHARLES'S ACKNOWLEDGMENTS

I THANK GOD FOR giving me braces to wear as a child, for the physical pain and social ridicule I endured, then, survived in the process, and for the many lessons in mercy and compassion You have taught me through it all. You are the only true and living God. Thank You for the gift of Your Son Jesus and the boundless forgiveness and compassion You extend to me every day.

Thanks to my mother for taking me to the library often and to my father for letting me use his typewriter at the age of nine years old to start a novel. Thanks to my wife, Dorothy, for more than two decades of enduring my dangerous lifestyle when most women would not have stayed around for such an experience. You kept the home fires burning and when I came home with blood on my clothes you would always ask, "Yours or theirs?" You cracked me up! Thanks, also, for taking it all in stride when I am out investigating human trafficking undercover in spas and massage parlors. Thanks for your trust and support.

Thanks to *all* of my children and my grandson for the love you demonstrate even when I don't get to hear you say it in words.

Now to many of my friends along the way — thanks to Dillon Burroughs; Bruce Ladebu; Lee Grady; Greg Hearn; Clay Hearn; Gary Moon; Chris Maxwell; Robyn Keeler; Sara Ray; Georgia Legg-Grady; Bruce and Melanie Adams; Megan Powell; Amy Davenport; Trevor Lanier; Joey Davis; Bishop Ron Carpenter Sr.; Rev. Chris Thompson; Rev. Talmadge Gardner; Rev. Doug Beacham; Rev. Gary Burd; Tim Vickery; Bobby Brooks; Wanda Phillips; Mark Palmer; Kayla Ray; Laura Ray; Rev. Warren Selman and family; Kelly Wright; US Congressman Paul D. Broun, MD; Georgia State Senator Renee Unterman; Mary Frances Bowley; Chong Kim; Lynn Latham; Sujo John; Mary and Ron Harold; Dorothy Wharton, my tenth-grade journalism teacher at TR Miller High School; Seth Edmonds for friendship, transcribing interviews, and really good coffee.

And to those in the following organizations — Mercy Movement, LifeSprings Resources, the International Pentecostal Holiness Church (IPHC), Evangelism USA, Mission: M25, Wellspring Living, Home of Hope-Texas, and New Hope Publishers.

DILLON'S ACKNOWLEDGMENTS

FIRST, I WANT to thank my wife, Deborah, whose love and support stand far beyond any other person on this planet. My children — Ben, Natalie, and Audrey — also provide the inspiration behind much of what I do. I love them and the hope they offer for a better tomorrow. Ben, already a published author at age eight; Natalie, designing the next generation's art; and Audrey, reminding us to pray even at the age of two — they are already on their own paths to change the world.

Beyond my family, I thank those of you who read this book, support it, share it, and live its principles. I pray for my readers daily, knowing that my words will ultimately be measured by the actions of you who read and apply them.

Specifically, to Colt, Josh, Ethan, and the Project Freedom team, thank you for your prayers and loyal friendship. Likewise, my friends at Woodland Park, the Ankerberg Theological Research Institute (ATRI), Tennessee Temple University, and FBC of North Terre Haute always encourage me.

To Dorothy Martin, both my mother-in-law and prayer partner, thank you for interceding on my behalf for well over a decade. Your rewards in heaven will be great.

Many organizations and ministries have helped along the way, most notably in my personal life have been Home of Hope-Texas, the Rescue Project, ALERT Ministries in Dallas, Mission of Hope Haiti, Mercy Movement, the Children's Rescue Initiative, the HOME Foundation, and DC Stop Modern Slavery. Likewise, my academic heroes in the antislavery effort, including Kevin Bales and his team at Free the Slaves, Aaron Cohen, the Not for Sale Campaign, Stop the Traffik, Traffick911 (Dallas-Ft. Worth), Coalition to Abolish Slavery & Trafficking (CAST)-LA, Polaris Project, Streetlight Phoenix, and Girls Educational & Mentoring Services (GEMS)-New York.

Finally and foremost, glory to God my Creator who strengthens my hands for this work.

NOTE ON SOURCES

To protect identities, some names, locations, and other details have been changed.

CHAPTER 1

YES, SLAVERY STILL EXISTS

D★I★L★L★O★N

SLAVERY STILL EXISTS.

On every continent but Antarctica, slavery is alive and well in the twenty-first century. According to David Batstone, author of *Not for Sale — The Return of the Global Slave Trade and How We Can Fight It*, more than *30 million* slaves live in our world today.[1]

Surprised? I know I was when I first discovered this information. I had known from news headlines that sex slavery took place in Southeast Asia, where groups such as the International Justice Mission (IJM) had been working to end slavery once and for all. But I thought our world was actually close to ending slavery.

I was wrong.

Thirty million people are more than double the number of victims who were transported during the entire transatlantic slave trade, by some estimates. Of course, there are far more people on the planet today, but put in these terms, we should be disturbed and ready to create positive change.

My one relief in years past had been, "Good thing there aren't any slaves in the US." We are the land of the free. The home of the brave.

It would not be until 2009, upon researching child slavery in Haiti after my second visit to the country, that I uncovered an ugly truth — slavery is alive and well in the United States. In fact, the United States is one of the top three destination points for trafficked victims, along with Japan and Australia, according to the Coalition to Abolish Slavery & Trafficking (CAST).[2] As antitrafficking advocate Christine Buckley notes:

> *American schoolkids are taught that slavery was wiped out with the Confederacy in 1865. But today it is a mounting international menace — the dark side, many believe, of globalization and the Internet explosion. Not to be confused with smuggling (which is always transnational and includes those who consent to the process), human trafficking implies the use of force, fraud or coercion and often involves ongoing exploitation. According to the Department of Health and Human Services, it is tied with the illegal-arms industry as the second-largest illegal business in the world, after drug dealing.[3]*

According to the nonprofit organization Free the Slaves, slavery happens in nearly every country of the world, and the US and Europe are not immune. Research that Free the Slaves conducted with the University of California, Berkeley, found documented cases of slavery and human trafficking in more than 90 cities across the United States.[4] According to the FBI, an estimated 15,000 to 18,000 people trafficked into the United States *each year*.[5] At any given time, conservative estimates indicate there are approximately 50,000 American slaves, not including tens of thousands of *Americans* involved in forced prostitution and domestic minor sex trafficking[6] (also known as child prostitution, impacting at least 100,000 children per year, according to Shared Hope International).[7] This is a number larger than the entire population of a US ZIP Code and perhaps larger than the population of the entire town in which you live. Though slavery is a hidden crime and no exact figures exist, Americans certainly have a tremendous responsibility to help the vast number of people living within slavery today *inside our own borders.*

That said, some areas of the country deal with the issue more than others. For example, in 2004 the FBI reported a case in Texas in which up to 100 people per week were being smuggled into the United States, with many held in slave conditions, working for no pay.[8] In terms of international trafficking via airports, cities with busy international airports such as Atlanta and Los Angeles rank high. In forced prostitution, Las Vegas is often cited. Sweatshops are frequently mentioned in New York cases, while California and the Southeast are prime areas for agricultural slavery. Domestic servants can be found nationwide, but are more often noted in Washington, D.C., and New York City. Regardless, as this book will show, no city and no community are immune.

In addition, slavery influences the global economy, ranging from the food we eat to the clothes we wear each day. According to the Free the Slaves Web site, "Slaves harvest cocoa in the Ivory Coast, make charcoal used to produce steel in Brazil, weave carpets in India — the list goes on." Since these products are in the stores we shop, and make their way into our homes, we should be concerned.[9]

In this chapter, we will take some time to help define modern slavery and human trafficking, and the various forms that exist. From there, we'll take you on a journey through our investigations of human trafficking, beginning where we live and extending across the country on an unforgettable journey that has only increased our resolve to help people in every American community be able to say to human trafficking, "Not in my town."

WHAT THE TITLE MEANS

First, we must define what we mean by our title, *Not in My Town*. What began as a goal has become a phrase with multiple meanings in our consultations with individuals, community groups, and churches. Our original goal was that "not in my town" would be the battle cry of individuals who choose to stand against human trafficking and modern slavery in their own communities. Yet as we've shared on this issue, we've experienced two other uses of the phrase. First, "not in my town" has been a response by many listeners who claim slavery does not exist where they live. A level of unbelief exists as it did in my own life at one point. We have been taught repeatedly that slavery ended after the Civil War. It doesn't exist, and if it does, it only exists "somewhere else." But in any sizable community this myth no longer works. We can quickly use the Internet or local publications to point out areas only minutes away where sex services can be purchased from those likely brought from another country and forced into the sex trade against their will. With a bit more searching or through public tools such as SlaveryMap.org, we can share cases close to home, creating looks of dread and disbelief among those in the audiences during our presentations.

For example, early in our research, Charles and I met at a café in the northwest suburbs of Atlanta to discuss upcoming plans when I first showed him the new tool I had found on SlaveryMap.org. We tested it and found a case of forced slave labor at a familiar restaurant only minutes away. Yet most people in the café where we were sitting likely had no idea these crimes had taken place in their own community.

The other, less frequent, "not in my town" responses we have run into have been from a few people who are uninterested in discussing modern slavery at all. Even if it *does* exist, they don't want to know about it. These cases are particularly frustrating, as if shielding our eyes makes the problem go away. This head-in-the-sand approach is one we have little patience with, as our goal is to help people in American communities stand against modern slavery in their local areas until those areas are slave-free. We firmly believe such efforts by you and others at the local level can make this a reality.

THE TERMS DEFINED

Next, we must also define terms when we discuss slavery and especially human trafficking. We want to be clear that this does not include people who are underpaid at their jobs or employees who feel mistreated by their employer for not letting them off during the holidays.

Simply defined, slavery is forcing someone to work with no pay beyond subsistence. As one leading advocate has defined it, slavery is "a relationship in which one person is controlled by violence through violence, the threat of violence, or psychological coercion, has lost free will and free movement, is exploited commercially, and is paid nothing beyond subsistence."[10]

In the US, the Department of Health and Human Services (HHS) powers the Rescue & Restore campaign, which seeks to identify and help trafficking victims. The department's extensive research points out that, "Human trafficking is a form of modern-day slavery. Victims of human trafficking are young children, teenagers, men and women." These individuals are "subjected to force, fraud, or coercion, for the purpose of sexual exploitation or forced labor."

The department's overview of this topic also states that after drug dealing, there are two criminal industries tied for the number two spot: human trafficking and arms dealing. Human trafficking is the fastest growing criminal industry. Many trafficking victims are forced into prostitution or the sex entertainment industry. Others are victims of labor exploitation, such as "domestic servitude, restaurant work, janitorial work, sweatshop factory work, and migrant agricultural work."

Victims are enslaved by traffickers through various techniques. According to HHS, some traffickers lock up their victims, but more frequently, they use less obvious techniques, including:

- *Debt bondage: financial obligations, honor-bound to satisfy debt*
- *Isolation from the public: limiting contact with outsiders and making sure that any contact is monitored or superficial in nature*
- *Isolation from family members and members of their ethnic and religious community*
- *Confiscation of passports, visas and/or identification documents*
- *Use or threat of violence toward victims and/or families of victims*
- *The threat of shaming victims by exposing circumstances to family*
- *Telling victims they will be imprisoned or deported for immigration violations if they contact authorities*
- *Control of the victims' money (e.g., holding their money for "safe-keeping")* [11]

Individuals enslaved by debt bondage are usually forced to pay transportation fees into the destination countries. They are often unaware that their debts are usually legally unenforceable and that it is illegal for traffickers to dictate how they have to pay off their debts. A cycle of debt is created: victims must pay for living expense, initial transportation expenses, fines for missing daily service quotas of service or for simply complaining. HHS notes that, "Most trafficked victims rarely see the money they are supposedly earning and may not even know the specific amount of their debt. Even if the victims sense that debt bondage is unjust, it is difficult for them to find help because of language, social, and physical barriers that keep them from obtaining assistance."[12]

HOW THE UN DEFINES TRAFFICKING

The *United Nations Protocol to Prevent, Suppress and Punish Trafficking in Persons, especially Women and Children*, defines trafficking in persons as:

> *The recruitment, transportation, transfer, harboring or receipt of persons, by means of threat or use of force or other forms of coercion, of abduction, of fraud, of deception, of the abuse of power or of a position of vulnerability or of the giving or receiving of payments or benefits to achieve the consent of a person having control over another person, for the purpose of exploitation. Exploitation shall include, at a minimum, the exploitation of the prostitution of others or other forms of sexual exploitation, forced labor or services, slavery or practices similar to slavery, servitude or the removal of organs.*

The Trafficking Victims Protection Act of 2000 (TVPA) was passed in October of 2000 and made human trafficking a federal crime. Its purpose was to "prevent human trafficking overseas, to protect victims and help them rebuild their lives in the US, and to prosecute traffickers of humans under federal penalties." Before this act, there was no comprehensive federal law meant to protect trafficking victims or to prosecute traffickers.[13]

The Trafficking Victims Protection Act of 2000 (TVPA) defines "Severe Forms of Trafficking in Persons" as:

- SEX TRAFFICKING: *the recruitment, harboring, transportation, provision, or obtaining of a person for the purpose of a commercial sex act, in which a commercial sex act is induced by force, fraud, or coercion, or in which the person forced to perform such an act is under the age of 18 years; or*

- LABOR TRAFFICKING: *the recruitment, harboring, transportation, provision, or obtaining of a person for labor or services, through the use of force, fraud or coercion for the purpose of subjection to involuntary servitude, peonage, debt bondage or slavery.*

Some confusion often exists between the terms "human trafficking" and "human smuggling." To be clear, there is a difference. Human smuggling involves people who consent to smuggling, enter a nation illegally, and involves the crossing of borders. Human trafficking, on the other hand, can be either within a nation or transnational. It can also begin with a situation in which the individual enters a country legally or even illegally by his or her own consent and is later involved in a form of forced labor. Trafficking may or may not include physical movement of a person, but always includes the *exploitation* of the person in some form of labor or sexual activity.[14]

SEX TRAFFICKING

Of the two forms of human trafficking identified above, sex trafficking receives the most attention (though it only makes up about half of the cases involving international trafficking into the US). Sex trafficking is a modern-day form of slavery in which "a commercial sex act is induced by force, fraud, or coercion, or in which the person induced to perform such an act is under the age of 18 years."[15] Enactment of the Trafficking Victims Protection Act of 2000 (TVPA) made sex trafficking a serious violation of federal law.

As defined by the TVPA, the term "commercial sex act" means any sex act on account of which anything of value is given to or received by any person. This also "recognizes that traffickers use psychological and well as physical coercion and bondage, and it defines coercion to include: threats of serious harm to or physical restraint against any person; any scheme, plan, or pattern intended to cause a person to believe that failure to perform an act would result in serious harm to or physical restraint against any person; or the abuse or threatened abuse of the legal process."[16]

Most, but not all, sex trafficking victims are women and girls. Common patterns for luring victims include:

- *A promise of a good job in another country*
- *A false marriage proposal turned into a bondage situation*
- *Being sold into the sex trade by parents, husbands, boyfriends*
- *Being kidnapped by traffickers*[17]

Sex traffickers frequently use debt bondage to control their victims. This illegal practice takes place when traffickers tell victims that they owe money (often related to the victims' expenses for living or being transported into the country) and that they must work off the debt. Starvation, confinement, physical abuse, rape, threats of violence to the victims and the victims' families, and forced drug use are just a few of the ways traffickers coerce their victims into servitude.[18]

Physical risks to sex trafficking victims include drug and alcohol addiction, traumatic brain injuries resulting in memory loss, dizziness, headaches, numbness, sexually transmitted diseases, sterility, miscarriages, and forced or coerced abortions. Victims may also suffer from shame, fear, distrust, self-hatred, suicidal thoughts, post-traumatic stress disorder, depression, and insomnia.[19]

The variety of *forms* within commercial sexual exploitation include prostitution, pornography, stripping, live-sex shows, mail-order brides, and sex tourism (further explained below). Sex trafficking can be found in both public and private locations, including massage parlors, spas, and strip clubs. Victims may begin by dancing or stripping in clubs and then be forced into prostitution and pornography.[20]

Two special forms of sex trafficking should also be mentioned at this point — the sex trafficking of children and sex tourism.

First, as explained in "The National Report on Domestic Minor Sex Trafficking," compiled by Shared Hope International:

> *Domestic minor sex trafficking (DMST) is the commercial sexual exploitation of American children within U.S. borders. It is the 'recruitment, harboring, transportation, provision, or obtaining of a*

person for the purpose of a commercial sex act' where the person is a U.S. citizen or lawful permanent resident under the age of 18 years. The age of the victim is the critical issue — there is no requirement to prove force, fraud, or coercion was used to secure the victim's actions. In fact, the law recognizes the effect of psychological manipulation by the trafficker, as well as the effect of threat of harm which traffickers/pimps use to maintain control over their young victims. DMST includes but is not limited to the commercial sexual exploitation of children through prostitution, pornography, and/or stripping. Experts estimate at least 100,000 American juveniles are victimized through prostitution in America each year. Domestic minor sex trafficking is child sex slavery, child sex trafficking, prostitution of children, commercial sexual exploitation of children (CSEC), and rape of a child.[21]

On the day this manuscript was completed, a massive child prostitution bust took place that rescued 69 children in cities all over the country. As reported by ABC News, "The undercover, 40-city operation was conducted by the FBI and state and local law enforcement over the weekend. Sixteen juveniles were taken off the streets in Seattle alone. In all, 884 people were arrested, including 99 men suspected of being pimps."[22]

Further, there is the controversial issue of sex tourism. As the name implies, sex tourism is traveling outside of the US with the intent of engaging in sexual activity. Sex tourism is legal in countries where prostitution is legal, but some countries have poorly enforced prostitution laws which increase *illegal* sex tourism. Sex tourists travel in order to have sexual relations with another individual, often for the exchange of money or presents. Sometimes, sex tourists engage in sex acts with children. A tourist who is having sex with a child (as defined by the host country) is committing a criminal offense in the host country, and also possibly in the country where the tourist is a citizen.[23] It is in this area especially that partners such as International Justice Mission have made significant progress, including several arrests of men traveling to Thailand and other parts of South Asia.[24] We will share more on various cities in the US regarding sex trafficking throughout other chapters in this book.

LABOR TRAFFICKING

Labor trafficking, the second major type of trafficking defined by the government, includes several forms as well. According to the HHS's fact sheet on human trafficking:

- BONDED LABOR, *or debt bondage is probably the least known form of labor trafficking today, and yet it is the most widely used method of enslaving people. Victims become bonded laborers when their labor is demanded as a means of repayment for a loan or service in which its terms and conditions have not been defined or in which the value of the victims' services as reasonably assessed is not applied toward the liquidation of the debt. The value of their work is greater than the original sum of money "borrowed."*

- FORCED LABOR *is a situation in which victims are forced to work against their own will, under the threat of violence or some other form of punishment, their freedom is restricted and a degree of ownership is exerted. Forms of forced labor can include domestic servitude; agricultural labor; sweatshop factory labor; janitorial, food service and other service industry labor; and begging.*

- CHILD LABOR *is a form of work that is likely to be hazardous to the health and/or physical, mental, spiritual, moral or social development of children and can interfere with their education. The International Labor Organization estimates worldwide that there are 246 million exploited children aged between 5 and 17 involved in debt bondage, forced recruitment for armed conflict, prostitution, pornography, the illegal drug trade, the illegal arms trade and other illicit activities around the world.*[25]

Labor trafficking victims are young children, teenagers, men, and women. Some enter the country legally on worker visas for domestic, "entertainment," computer, and agricultural work, while others enter illegally. Some take on legal occupations such as domestic, factory or construction work, while others are in illegal industries such as the drug and arms trade or panhandling. There is no one way to identify victims of labor trafficking, but here are some common patterns, according to HHS:

- *Victims are often kept isolated to prevent them from getting help. Their activities are restricted and are typically watched, escorted or guarded by associates of traffickers. Traffickers may "coach" them to answer questions with a cover story about being a student or tourist.*

- *Victims may be blackmailed by traffickers using the victims' status as an undocumented alien or their participation in an "illegal" industry. By threatening to report them to law enforcement or immigration officials, traffickers keep victims compliant.*

- *People who are trafficked often come from unstable and economically devastated places as traffickers frequently identify vulnerable populations characterized by oppression, high rates of illiteracy, little social mobility and few economic opportunities.*

- *Women and children are overwhelmingly trafficked in labor arenas because of their relative lack of power, social marginalization, and their overall status as compared to men.*[26]

These victims suffer from a variety of physical and mental health problems, some of which are listed here.

- *Various methods of forced labor expose victims of labor trafficking to physical abuse such as scars, headaches, hearing loss, cardiovascular/respiratory problems, and limb amputation. Victims of labor trafficking may also develop chronic back, visual and respiratory problems from working in agriculture, construction or manufacturing under dangerous conditions.*

- The psychological effects of torture are helplessness, shame and humiliation, shock, denial and disbelief, disorientation and confusion, and anxiety disorders including post-traumatic stress disorder (PTSD), phobias, panic attacks, and depression.

- Many victims also develop traumatic bonding, or Stockholm syndrome, which is characterized by cognitive distortions where reciprocal positive feelings develop between captors and their hostages. This bond is a type of human survival instinct and helps the victim cope with the captivity.

- Child victims of labor trafficking are often malnourished to the extent that they may never reach their full height, they may have poorly formed or rotting teeth, and later they may experience reproductive problems.[27]

WHERE DOES LABOR TRAFFICKING TAKE PLACE IN THE US?

- domestic servitude/worker cases (nannies, maids/housekeepers)
- landscaping
- nail salons
- restaurants
- industrial cleaning
- construction
- hospitality
- sales crews
- agriculture

SOURCE: THE POLARIS PROJECT[28]

According to 2004 research from Free the Slaves in collaboration with the Berkeley Human Rights Center, "At any given time ten thousand or more people are working as forced laborers in the United States. It is likely that the actual number reaches into the tens of thousands. Determining the exact number of victims, however, has proven difficult given the hidden nature of forced labor and the manner in which these figures are collected and analyzed."[29]

This research cited above mentioned one especially notable case that highlights the specific area of forced domestic labor within our nation's capital. In the case against the the Satias, two Cameroonian sisters and their husbands, two young Cameroonian girls, aged 14 and 17, were recruited to work as domestics in their Washington, D.C., homes:

> *"The girls were recruited with the promise of studying in the U.S. in exchange for providing child-care and domestic help. Once in the U.S., the domestic servants were confined to the Satias' homes, working in excess of fourteen hours a day without remuneration and under threat of violence and deportation. The younger survivor escaped in 1999 after two years of captivity. A year later the older survivor fled, after having been exploited for five years. In 2001 the Satia sisters and their husbands were charged with forced labor. Found guilty, they received criminal sentences ranging from five to nine years and were ordered to pay their victims over $100,000 in restitution."[30]*

HUMAN TRAFFICKING WORLDWIDE

- Number of countries identified as affected by human trafficking: 161.

  SOURCE: UN OFFICE ON DRUGS AND CRIME,
  Trafficking in Persons: Global Patterns: APRIL 2006.

- Total yearly profits generated by the human trafficking industry: $32 billion. $15.5 billion is made in industrialized countries; $9.7 billion in Asia.

  SOURCE: THE POLARIS PROJECT[31]

As noted in Free the Slaves' "Top 10 Facts About Modern Slavery," "Slavery is not legal anywhere but happens everywhere."[32] One final account points out how easily many fall into the trap of this modern evil:

> *I was 14 years old, and the way the pimp came at me was that at first I didn't even know he was a pimp. He came at me like a boyfriend. Yes, he was an older boyfriend but he cared about me. . . . Six months later he told me 'Let's run away together. We can have a beautiful house and family.' And I did believe him, and we ran away, and then the story changed and I met the other girls that he had in his stable. And I had to go out every night and work the streets — the alternative was being gang-raped by a group of pimps while everyone watched.*[33]

Though tragic, there is a shining hope in this story. The individual involved, Tina Frundt, founded Courtney's House, a sex trafficking aftercare home in our nation's capital. Rather than being defeated by the tragedy that destroyed this dark period of her life, Tina has not only survived but now cares for others held in bondage.

If she can, we can. I can. You can. Join us in our journey to stop modern slavery in the United States of America.

CHAPTER 2:

THE FIRST STEP: YOU ARE HERE

C☆H☆A☆R☆L☆E☆S & D☆I☆L☆L☆O☆N

CHARLES'S STORY

I SPENT MY 20s and 30s experimenting with dangerous living on a scale few men survive. At the age of 21, I was trained in nuclear counterterrorism and security techniques then protected special nuclear materials as well as the general public from a terror-related nuclear incident. Next, I parlayed my previous training into an executive and dignitary protection position for numerous sheiks, oil executives, billionaires, and the occasional member of the Saudi royal family.

I was recruited to work undercover for one of the many government contractors fighting President Reagan's War on Drugs. Though this was an adrenaline-pumping opportunity, I nearly lost my life and almost cost my family their lives one too many times, so I resigned and became a policeman in Houston for one of the city's 78 law enforcement agencies. There I hit the streets when a three-year war broke out among rival gangs over crack cocaine production, distribution, and sales. I worked patrol, burglary investigation, and spent time on a stakeout squad until a 1993 car accident with a drunk driver took me out of the action for the next six years.

By 2001 I was healed enough to get back into the fray. Early that year I flew to Venezuela to investigate human rights issues, Hugo Chavez's secret police, and the Venezuelan military's activities against Christians. During this time, the group I was working with organized pastors and aid workers to plan means for them to offer food, education, and medical services to those in need without direct help from the US due to Chavez's increasing anti-American policies.[1]

In 2002, at the request of my wife, I chose a simpler and quieter approach to life. We moved our family to rural northeast Georgia, where I have worked for a publisher as its marketing director. This evolved into producing network television for a company in Nashville and in Los Angeles. Everything remained quiet in this role until 2009 when we booked a member of the International Justice Mission (IJM) for a talk show to discuss the topic of human trafficking.

That day everything changed for me.

I determined that I was going to do something about the scourge of modern-day slavery, but what would I do?

What could I do?

After much soul searching and very little prayer (a mistake) I determined to offer my skills to work undercover for IJM somewhere in South Asia to uncover evidence of sexual slavery. I was ready to rescue some kids. I began telling very close friends about my decision, seeking moral support in the process. Then one of these friends asked what has proven to be a providential question: "Why are you going to South Asia to fight human trafficking and sexual slavery when the number one destination for such activities in the United States is right here in Atlanta?"

I was stunned.

Speechless.

After looking into my friend's claim, I readily found information from the US government and law enforcement officials that gave evidence to the veracity of his claim. This discovery marked an "about face" to educate myself about the broader problem of human trafficking and modern slavery. I promised God I would give Him a year dedicated to prayer, study, and investigation on the matter. *Not in My Town* is the result of this pilgrimage.

DILLON'S STORY

As a writer on issues of faith and culture, I'm always looking for a great story. After authoring or coauthoring over 20 books and editing many others, I had hit a period of fatigue that led to much prayer seeking future direction. One result of this process was a short-term trip to Port-au-Prince, Haiti, in June 2009 to visit an organization called Mission of Hope. A large operation, their 75-acre compound included a school of 1,200 students, a quality medical facility, an orphanage, food and water programs, and a vibrant church.

Though inspired and impressed by the efforts of the American and Canadian team changing lives in this region, it was a drive to the airport on our final day that would mark my future calling. To label our trip a "drive" is an overstatement. The ride was in the back of a caged delivery truck that resembled the numerous Haitian "tap-taps" used for public transportation across the country. The bumpy, exhaust-filled journey became an early morning hour of reflection concerning my time in the area. Many stops occurred along the way; one I will never forget. Outside a corrugated metal shack, a group of children were being forced to work, preparing items for sale at one of the many roadside markets. To watch a child being hit in the face was one of most agonizing experiences of my life. The message to the other children was also clear — submit or you're next.

These children are being treated like slaves, was the first thought to cross my mind. I knew something had to be done. God allowed me to witness that moment for a reason. During the rest of the drive, I peered more closely through the metal mesh covering our vehicle, spotting additional kids along the way who worked with a sense of hopelessness in their eyes. Many were the age of my son at the time, only seven years old.

Upon my return to the States, I immediately set out to research the child labor situation in Haiti. It did not take long to run into the oft-quoted statistic that there are more slaves in Haiti than any nation in the Western Hemisphere. In my mind, I had found my cause. I began supporting child development efforts in Haiti, telling everyone I could about the tragedy of humans being bought and sold less than a two-hour flight from Miami.

Called *restaveks*, a term meaning "be with," this social caste system traditionally includes a child being raised by someone other than the child's parents in return for housing, food, and education. In reality, these promises were rarely fulfilled. Rampant abuse, sexual misconduct, forced labor, and even occasional torture marks the existence of many. Per some estimates, as many as 250,000 Haitians live as *restaveks*. In 2010, UNICEF reported that approximately 250,000 children are victims of the practice.[2] One former restavek victim reported to CNN after the 2010 earthquake in Haiti that about 80 percent of Haiti's restavek children are girls, and thus vulnerable to sexual abuse and early pregancy.[3]

During this time, I read reports about modern slavery, learning it is now typically labeled human trafficking, including a special United Nations report on human rights violations that had been taking place in Haiti during the same week I had been in the country. This also helped explain the increased UN Peacekeeper presence during our travels. On a whim and perhaps out of zeal as a writer wanting to make a difference, I emailed the Swiss representative from the UN who had produced the report to share my experiences from visiting Haiti during the same time period she did. Sadly, my report was only one of a multitude filed regarding children exploited for profits that cost less than my morning cup of coffee.

At this point, I was fired up. Frankly, I was furious at the level of human injustice that would allow me the ability to fly to a neighboring nation and buy a *person* for only $50 in less than a day. At times, I was tempted to raise money to simply buy as many people as I could and set them free. I think I read the story of Moses in Exodus about 50 times during this period.

As I continued my learning through governmental reports, academic papers, and Web sites, I ran into an almost unbelievable statement — that modern slavery was taking place *in my own country*. It was only after confirming this disturbing fact through multiple sources that I could even accept this ugly truth. Simply put: there has never been a day in America's history without slavery. Laws had changed the status of the act, but had not ended slavery completely.

Why had I never heard about this? I read numerous books and periodicals each year and knew about slavery in Southeast Asia and parts of the developing world, but apparently not many people are excited to talk about slavery in their own backyard. It often takes a good bit of detective work to even find solid research on the issue. For the past decade, the US government has even issued a yearly report on human trafficking that ranks each nation according to its policies and practices. It wasn't until this past year that the US published details about our own country's record regarding human trafficking. Yes, we're on the "good list," unlike Haiti, India, or Thailand, but there are still 15,000 to 18,000 estimated people *per year* brought into the United States for forced labor.[4]

According to the insightful book *The Slave Next Door*, a rough conservative estimate is that approximately 50,000 people live in slavery in America *right now*,[5] not including the many *American citizens* forced into sex trafficking either as children or adults. As a hidden crime, there are no exact numbers of how many victims are actually in existence.

In terms of new headlines, it is often what is referred to as domestic minor sex trafficking (or DMST) that draws attention. What was once labeled child prostitution (any purchase or exchange of other goods for sex with a person under 18 years old) has been redefined more accurately as the forced sexual labor of children. DMST crimes have been the focus of popular films and investigative television reports, but the most credible organization fighting to draw public attention to the issue and stop this heinous act is Shared Hope International, a nonprofit founded by former Congresswoman Linda Smith following her observation of the sex trade in India.

Her most revealing research to date is the DMST Project, which provided assessments of DMST activities in over a dozen major US cities. The report's conclusions are summarized here:

- *At least 100,000 children are used in prostitution every year in the United States.*

- *The average age of entry into prostitution is 13 years old.*

- *Prostituted girls are often controlled by a pimp who recruits them into sex trafficking by posing as a boyfriend, caretaker, and protector.*

- *The three primary manifestations of child sex trafficking in America are: pimp-controlled prostitution, familial prostitution, and/or survival sex.*[6]

The sad truth is that with a simple public Internet search, I can find a person who has been brought into the US from another country *or from the US* and forced into prostitution and become their so-called client in a variety of sexual acts. The very thought sickens me. But as this book will show, the prevalence of this activity is far greater than most know. In a test of how closely I could find a "partner" for a person at one presentation, a hush came over the room as we discovered the location was within walking distance of where we were sitting. Sadly, I have been able to repeat this experiment with similar results across the country. In most major American cities, you could likely find a similar situation within a short walk or drive from your office.

For a safer example, you can take a look at SlaveryMap.org, a Web-based tool used to map human trafficking crimes in our nation. In the past two years, over 1,288 reports of human trafficking in the US have been reported. You can search your local area, neighboring communities, and entire state to determine how prevalent this social ill is to your home. We've contributed a few new cases ourselves since beginning our investigations, primarily based on cases we've known that had not yet been added to the list. As a user-contributed site (though moderated by a reputable antitrafficking organization), its information is based on what people have reported, meaning numerous additional examples exist that go unlisted.[7]

I currently live in Chattanooga, just beyond the Atlanta metro area on the north side of the Georgia state line in Tennessee. Considered a conservative community, most would not think human trafficking is a major issue of concern. However, on the contrary, SlaveryMap.org notes the nearest report to my home is 12 minutes away and involved a forced labor situation.

This revelation has had a profound impact on me. No longer can I drive past a billboard for a massage parlor or certain hotels and not think about what might be taking place. No longer can I buy products without considering whether they include slave labor. No longer can I passively allow Internet companies to market the serial rape of women and children. No longer can I tolerate ATM machines and other financial or leasing services provided to known trafficking locations. No longer can I tolerate "community papers" that include advertisements for so-called escorts and other cover-ups for what sometimes includes a person forced into the sex trade. No longer can I tolerate abuses of immigrant workers who are at times forced to work without pay and under threat of violence. Not in my town.

The message of this book is clear: slavery is alive and well in America. That's the bad news. In fact, it's tragic. The good news is that it can be reduced and perhaps stopped in this generation. But ending trafficking in our nation will only occur when you and I and people in churches, schools, college campuses, workplaces, law enforcement, and government *all* stand up and demand the end of trafficking in all forms *at the local level*.

Already, much is taking place. More than 40 states (43 as of the time of this writing) have approved legislation to provide much stiffer penalties for modern-day slave owners and operators. The number of cases tackling this thorny societal evil continues to grow, a positive move since it sets legal precedent to deter demand, allows some victims to escape trafficking, and brings media attention to the topic. Further, one of the nation's most commonly mentioned online sources of trafficking activity, Craigslist.com, announced after years of grassroots efforts to stop its erotic ads section, that it would comply and remove all such postings in this category. Other Web sites, due to similar pressures, are beginning to make similar changes. In 2010, our friends from the DC Stop Modern Trafficking group, along with others, helped petition *The Washington Post* to remove ads for massage parlors, a common location for trafficking activities.[8] Other national newspapers are investigating or implementing similar measures.

Yet much work remains. Sadly, the main voices and organizations fighting human trafficking in America at this point have not primarily been from the church. Rather, ordinary citizens have discovered the problem and are doing something about it. Partnering together, people of faith in this nation, representing well over 300,000 congregations, have the influence to put a huge dent in this issue. As the African American civil rights movement of the twentieth century found success when Christians stood up to the moral evil of racism and segregation, I firmly believe the anti-trafficking movement of the twenty-first century will not achieve a high level of success in ending American trafficking until Christians and other people of faith join the movement.

In a providential move of God, I reconnected with my friend Charles in late summer 2009. As I shared what had been taking place in my life on this issue, I could almost feel his smile on the other end of the line. He had recently begun the process to form an organization to equip people to stand against human trafficking across America. In a moment I could only describe as a "God thing" we vowed to join together to expand the impact of people of faith who would be the ones to help shift the action of the church into reducing trafficking in their own communities.

What began as a moment in the back of a truck on the way to Port-au-Prince for me and conversations with IJM staff members for Charles has led to what we now call the Mercy Movement. This book represents our desire to educate and motivate people of faith to join in our efforts to boldly stand against human trafficking and modern slavery, proclaiming, "Not in my town."

CHAPTER 3:

WHERE TO BEGIN: JUST LOOK OUT THE DOOR—ATLANTA, GEORGIA

C☆H☆A☆R☆L☆E☆S

MY YEAR DEDICATED to prayer, study, and investigation of human trafficking and sexual slavery began in Atlanta.

There's no place like home.

I love the city of Atlanta.

The ATL.

Now honesty requires that I inform you that I do not live within the city limits of Atlanta. As mentioned, I live in the country north of town, but the Greater Atlanta area is steadily growing my way every day and before you know it, without ever moving, I'll be there! That said, I drive into the city every chance I get if only to reconnect on weekday afternoons, weekends, or at night. If you can't find me at home or somewhere around my little town, chances are I'm in Atlanta.

My favorite time to be in the city is at night. Three things make nighttime special in Atlanta.

In the late spring the heat and humidity are downright tolerable. It's the perfect time to catch a Braves game. It's a tradition in Atlanta to dress well (women often wear big hats and sundresses), attend the game with friends, and enjoy pleasant conversation while sharing ballpark food and rooting the home team to victory.

The High Museum is another favorite. The finest art exhibitions in the world always seem to make their way to Atlanta, the self-proclaimed Capital of the South. Friday night is jazz night at the High where I can listen to great music and view works of art from around the world until 10:00 P.M.

No night out in Atlanta would be complete without eating the local fare — my very favorite barbeque can be found at Fat Matt's on Piedmont Avenue. When I arrive at Matt's, I hang out for a while listening to the live blues music. Plus, I'm always available to sit in with the band singing and playing my harmonica for a few songs. I love the music, but the problem is that from the moment I enter the door, the aroma of barbeque and sweet potato pie coming from the kitchen assaults my senses until I can no longer wait.

Then I place my order . . .

Yes sir . . . can I please have a full slab of ribs with extra sauce

Huge scoop of potato salad

A big ole bowl of baked beans

Iced tea

Then please tell me you have some sweet potato pie left, 'cause you *"fix it"* the way my mama *"fixed it!"*

I never allow my formal education to get in the way of proudly placing my order using my Southern vernacular!

With my order placed, I take a booth outside the restaurant, even if I have to wait for one. Once seated, I close my eyes for a moment and breathe in the clean spring air, pausing to have its way with my mind, taking me to places both present and past as red, blue, and yellow neon lights perform a rhythmic dance on my ceramic plate.

PASSING TIME ON PIEDMONT

There's something a bit magical about eating Fat Matt's sauce-laden ribs outdoors, especially in the fall. My nighttime visits to Piedmont Avenue have always centered on music, atmosphere, and barbeque with all the "fixins." Yet lately I have discovered that some people on the opposite end of the avenue are focused on travel to Piedmont for another pastime — sex for hire.

In recent years the area has become the infamous home to a number of Asian spas and massage parlors that are open 24/7. Like many of these establishments across the Atlanta metro, some of the Piedmont AMPs (Asian massage parlors as they are called by sexual tourists) exhibit traits that are often associated with sexual slavery and human trafficking. To be clear, let me go ahead and state what both my critics and the criminal element do not want revealed — organized crime is absolutely involved. We'll talk more about that later.

While you can easily find foreign-based ethnic and domestic organized crime groups profiting from various criminal activities throughout the city, no ethnic group in Atlanta (or the entire state of Georgia for that matter) has a firm grip on massage parlor prostitution like those from South Korea. From east Tennessee, throughout the Carolinas, and in all of Georgia to the Florida line, Korean-organized crime, whether alone or working as vendors for Chinese organized crime, profits more from prostitution and human trafficking in spas and massage parlors than all other trafficking rings combined.

ATLANTA'S LONG HISTORY IN SLAVERY

But sexual slavery is not new to the Peach State. Prostitution is an inescapable part of history in Atlanta. Long before Margaret Mitchell's *Gone with the Wind* introduced us to prostitute and madam Belle Watling, real Civil War-era soiled doves, as they were called then, worked in Atlanta brothels without fear of interference from law enforcement. Human trafficking was the order of the day and legal prior to and during the war. African American slave women were often forced against their will to perform sex acts for their masters and sometimes made to work in brothels. Now, 145 years later, things have changed and yet in some ways they are still the same.

Slavery still exists in Atlanta today. In the form of sexual slavery in spas and massage parlors, women and underage girls are forced to work as prostitutes by pimps who advertise openly on public Web sites. Somewhere in Atlanta a person works as a household servant under conditions equal to slavery. Farm workers pass through our city by bus on their way to harvest yet another crop, but since they are charged so much for their entry into our country by the people who hire them out, their wages always seem to equal their expenses.

None of the individuals I have described above is perfectly free to leave at any time. They are slaves and by definition have masters who prevent them from leaving. That is when these individuals often discover they have become a slave. When you can no longer say no and when your freedom to choose whether to stay or to go has been taken away, that is the moment slavery begins. As the great abolitionist and former slave Frederick Douglass once wrote, "I didn't know I was a slave until I found out I couldn't do the things I wanted."[1]

MY MISSION

I took a year to observe and investigate human trafficking across the US, but I spent most of that year looking into the modern slavery problem in my favorite city, what some consider the American epicenter for human trafficking: Atlanta.

I looked at it.

I stared at it.

I faced it through the eyes of the man that I am, a man with eyes trained at great cost to see vice and crime where others are blind to its existence. But I didn't know *how* to begin. I needed guidance and direction, so I searched Atlanta and spotted a bit of light emanating from 449 Auburn Avenue NE, the address where you'll find the tribute to and resting place of my greatest hero, Dr. Martin Luther King Jr. In 1968, I was a six-year-old boy living in Laurel, Mississippi, surrounded by institutional segregation. The day after Dr. King was killed the news media played excerpts from his many public appearances, in particular his "I have a dream" speech in Washington, D.C.

His words made sense to me.

The words he spoke marked the first time in my short life I'd ever heard an adult voice the way I felt inside about race and civil rights issues.

Unfortunately, the immediate hope his words kindled in me was short-lived because the news reporter soon explained my new hero had been shot dead in Memphis, Tennessee, by an assassin's bullet. Dr. King's words have always been a light to my path whenever I needed direction. So as I sought my way I looked to his writings and speeches. Soon I found words to provide direction for my quest.

> *If you want to be important — wonderful.*
> *If you want to be recognized — wonderful.*
> *If you want to be great — wonderful.*
> *But recognize that he who is greatest among you shall be your servant. That's a new definition of greatness. The thing that I like about it: by giving that definition of greatness, it means that everybody can be great, because everybody can serve.*[2]

The answer I was seeking was simple — I could be a servant to the slave. I determined to do something about human trafficking, whatever the cost to me personally or professionally. If doing so made me unpopular with politicians or those within organized religion, so be it. Should my commitment cause me to be arrested or harassed by law enforcement officials I embarrass for revealing their lack of belief in the existence of human trafficking in America, so be it. If my investigations, writing, and publicity about modern slavery caused criminal elements to consider me a target, then I would stand undaunted.

My new mission became to serve victims of human trafficking by:

- *exposing anyone who profits from slavery using every legal, moral, ethical, and nonviolent means at my disposal;*

- *seeking to bring freedom to modern-day slaves in the US;*

- *exposing any individual or group who seeks to deny the existence of modern-day slavery and the involvement of organized criminal elements which make it possible;*

- *educating churches, civic organizations, law enforcement, corporations, students, and individuals about the reality of modern-day slavery;*

- *marginalizing those individuals and groups who would deny the victims of human trafficking dignity, legal assistance, relief, healing, or help up from their circumstances.*

LEGISLATING HUMAN TRAFFICKING

About five years ago Georgia enacted an anti-human trafficking law. It began with a very slow impact on the commercial sexual exploitation of children across the state, but according to state and federal law enforcement officials, successes have shot up quickly in the past two years, particularly in Atlanta. Why? In April 2006, the Georgia General Assembly passed the measure, and the governor readily signed SB 529, known commonly as the Georgia Security and Immigration Compliance Act. One of the good things this bill did was to create a new segment to the crimes and offense section of the Georgia Code, establishing two new human trafficking offenses: one for trafficking a person for labor servitude, and another for trafficking a person for sexual servitude.

This new Georgia state law was derived in part from the Model Anti-Trafficking Criminal Statute as promoted for use by the US Department of Justice. However, it does not duplicate that model's real meaning, and in fact, it fails to properly define its key terms. The new section, O.C.G.A. § 16-5-46, does not define sexual servitude of a minor as a separate offense, but rather includes it under the broader offense of trafficking a person for sexual servitude. Sexual servitude is defined by the law as:

(A) Any sexually explicit conduct . . . for which anything of value is directly or indirectly given, promised to, or received by any person, which conduct is induced or obtained by coercion or deception or which conduct is induced or obtained from a person under the age of 18 years; or

(B) Any sexually explicit conduct. . . which is performed or provided by any person, which is induced or obtained by coercion or deception or which conduct is induced or obtained from a person under the age of 18 years.[3]

Unfortunately, this definition is too broad and too narrow thereby weakening the law. I find it too broad because neither "induced nor obtained" are ever really defined. Webster's defines *induced* as (1) "to move by persuasion or influence; or (2) to call forth or bring about by influence or stimulation." Using such a broad definition, Part (B) could be read to encompass all sexual activity involving a juvenile, because nearly all "consensual" sexual activity is brought about by either persuasion or stimulation. The effect of this approach to the law would be to replace the statutory rape statute, making sex with a minor a felony in all instances including when a minor has sex with another minor. While I do not recommend that minors should have sex at anytime, the flaws in the statute's authorship begin to reveal themselves under this type of scrutiny.

On the other hand, the definition is too narrow because if "induced or obtained" are given a narrow reading, some young prostitutes would not be considered trafficking victims. Those prostitutes under 18 who "voluntarily" work without a pimp and proactively make offers to "Johns" (purchasers of sexual services) might be excluded. Also, a narrow reading of the statute as originally passed would mean that not every "John" would be guilty of human trafficking and thereby negate the law's original purpose.

According to the "Final Report of the Commercial Sexual Exploitation of Minors Joint Study Commission," a public document prepared and published by the Senate research office in 2008 and supplied to me by the office of Georgia State Senator Renee Unterman, co-chair of the Commission, reads:

Georgia's anti-human trafficking statute was enacted in 2006 as part of the Georgia Security and Immigration Compliance Act. The statute creates two criminal offenses: trafficking a person for labor servitude; and trafficking a person for sexual servitude. The offense of trafficking a person for sexual servitude could potentially be used

> to prosecute pimps or johns who sexually exploit children and covers sexually explicit conduct 'which is induced or obtained by coercion or deception or which conduct is induced or obtained from a person under the age of 18 years.' According to the Barton Clinic, however, the statute as currently written is overly broad, possibly hindering its use as a prosecutorial tool. The meaning of 'induced or obtained,' as used in the definition of 'sexual servitude' is never delineated, and could be considered so broad as to cover a spectrum of activities that are not necessarily true instances of commercial sexual exploitation. Moreover, the definition of sexual servitude as 'sexually explicit conduct which . . . is induced or obtained by a person under the age of 18 years' could be broadly construed to criminalize all sexual activity with a person under 18, effectively raising the age of consent in Georgia to 18.[4]

Regardless of the law's inadequacies, the most shameful fact on the matter is that from the time the measure was signed into law in 2006, it took local, state, and federal law enforcement *two years* to use the state statute to prosecute the first cases against individuals accused of human trafficking.

Regardless of circumstances, minor prostitutes are victims and should never be prosecuted or treated as criminals. They should instead *always* be treated as victims, because only some form of circumstantial or physical victimization would cause a minor to engage in prostitution, regardless of comments made in the press by certain misguided political and religious leaders in the state of Georgia who deny the existence of prostitution and human trafficking in the state of Georgia.

A leading member of the most prominent Christian public policy organization in Georgia once called me in response to a magazine article I wrote and during the phone call stated, "I think the whole problem is bad girls. No one is being forced to be a prostitute in the state of Georgia. These girls just like sex and they think they can make a lot of money working as a prostitute so they do so . . . Anyway, I don't believe anything I cannot see so I believe in human trafficking about as much as I believe in 'Big Foot.'"

During the 2010 legislative session, State Senator Renee Unterman sought to pass legislation that in short would have recognized all underage prostitutes as victims. Previously Unterman was known to have aided a variety of Christian conservative causes, including the "Choose Life" state license plate and the state requirement that women seeking an abortion must be offered a sonogram beforehand.

Renee Unterman, the only woman in the Georgia State Senate, was seen as the darling of the religious and political right.

Was is the operative word.

Much of the support she once knew from religious conservatives stopped when Senator Unterman took up the cause of underage prostitution. Some conservative church groups and conservative Christian policy organizations, along with a few former politicians and political pundits, made pointed attacks against Unterman's legislation and character in statements made online and in *The Atlanta Journal Constitution*, proclaiming her legislation to be the decriminalization of underage prostitution in the Georgia.

As the author states regarding various reactions, "Spare-the-rod arguments were plentiful. 'The threat of arrest, public humiliation and a police record has scared straight many minors and adults,' said Sue Ella Deadwyler, who writes a Christian conservative newsletter. 'Arrest is a valuable life-saving tool that must continue.'"

Why? Because her Senate Bill 304 would declare that boys and girls under age 16 shouldn't be charged with prostitution, but diverted to treatment or therapy. Her biggest supporters were actually from the media, where the *Atlanta Journal Constitution* hailed Unterman's measure as "an attempt to bring a certain legal and moral consistency to Georgia law."[5]

The debate over this issue blew me away and proved to me that many suburban evangelicals don't have a clue about what is happening outside or inside their cloistered neighborhoods and social groups.

Many Christians believe (as I do) that a teenager should not be able to have an abortion, especially without parental consent when they are minors and therefore, not responsible enough to make such a serious and final life choice. Yet many Christians who share this belief are the same people who believe underage minor prostitutes should be prosecuted as adult prostitutes and not treated as victims under the law.

A more honest analysis is found in the report "Hidden in Plain View: The Commercial Sexual Exploitation of Girls in Atlanta"[6] along with The Schapiro Group's "Men Who Buy Sex with Adolescent Girls: A Scientific Research Study,"[7] both of which clearly paint a picture of Atlanta as a place where conventioneers, business travelers, and even sexual tourists travel to exploit minor prostitutes, many of whom are victims of human trafficking.

> *Johns get connected with a pimp via the Internet, fly in for the purpose of sex with a young girl or boy who is waiting in a hotel, apartment or office, then fly home for dinner.*
>
> — CHIEF JUDGE SANFORD JONES,
> Fulton County (Georgia) Juvenile Court[8]

Fortunately not all were against Senator Unterman's bill. Her supporters included State Representative Doug Collins (R-Gainesville). "I'm a pastor and I have no problem with the [Unterman] bill," Collins was quoted as saying in *The Atlanta Journal Constitution* on February 3, 2010.[9] He's the kind of guy, both politically and spiritually, I can stand together with on this issue.

PROMOTING PROSTITUTION

So as I made my way across the city of Atlanta studying the problem of pimps, prostitution, massage parlors, and spas, I learned that the media plays a major role in promoting prostitution in the city using Craigslist.com, Backpage.com, and local papers like *Creative Loafing*. An alternative newsweekly publication, *Creative Loafing* boasts a circulation of 100,000, available for free throughout the greater Atlanta area in 1,700 locations such as restaurants, convenience stores, bars, adult bookstores, adult video stores, "smoke shops" (stores where drug paraphernalia is purchased), and many other places. For years the publication has been known for featuring local news stories, national news, as well as the ebb and flow of societal and cultural change in Atlanta and across the country as a whole. The publication is also known for advertisements for concerts, restaurants, and comedy clubs. Further, it is commonly known among Atlanta locals that the publication serves as the city's mouthpiece for a plethora of conservative hating, Republican-bashing, and Christian-crucifying activism.

I support this publication not for its content but because of my belief in the freedom of the press and free speech. Of course that does not mean that all free speech is intelligent speech or that all press is equal to good journalism. There is not much journalistic integrity in a publication which prints adult classified ads meant to offer women as prostitutes. I once read in the publication an ad placed by a pregnant woman who claimed to have worked previously at the infamous Moonlite BunnyRanch, a legal brothel in Nevada made famous by an HBO television series. In the ad the woman clearly offered herself for sexual liaisons, and this ad is only one of many like it. On a regular basis, the adult classified section in *Creative Loafing* hosts ads for adult spas and massage parlors, escort services, strip clubs, adult book and video stores, as well as individuals who offer their services for so-called escorts. There is more than anecdotal evidence that *Creative Loafing* has been or could easily be used by anyone seeking to traffic underage women for the purposes of prostitution, but they are certainly not alone.

In the past, *Creative Loafing*, Craigslist.com, and Backpage.com have all featured ads with descriptions for females who are "petite," "young," "barely legal," "just turned 18," and other descriptions that would not be appropriate for this writing. All of these descriptions are tried and true catchphrases for describing underage girls who are being trafficked either by pimps or organized criminal elements.

I have not discovered any systems in place at *Creative Loafing* or Backpage.com which might safeguard against promoting underage girls or women who are being prostituted through the use of and for the profit of their respective organizations. (NOTE: Craigslist.com recently made updates by dropping their "erotic ads" section in the United States due to public pressure, but some have noted the continued use of other categories featuring similar practices and the fact that the change only currently applies to the US.) Be aware that *Creative Loafing*, Craigslist.com, and Backpage.com are only three of numerous for-profit media outlets available for customers to find women and girls being prostituted through spas and massage parlors, through pimps, and individually.

MY FIRSTHAND RESEARCH

Studying the Internet and reading newspapers, however, did not provide enough understanding of Atlanta's economy of prostitution and the human trafficking it creates. Rather than relying on secondary sources, I hit the streets and returned to the "field craft" from my days undercover. Atlanta is not unlike many other urban centers in the United States in that it is very common to find yourself driving through a very "good" part of town and within moments roll into a "bad" part of town.

By "good" we often mean a community featuring new hotels and office buildings competing to outshine the ones built next to them, and all its residents are filled with hope. By "bad" we often think of a community where poverty, crime, and urban blight have polluted the landscape and infected its people with despair on a generational scale. Social ills exist in every part of its environment waiting to be ingested by those caught in the near inescapable atmosphere.

Next, however, you would expect me to write that the "bad" neighborhood would be the ideal breeding ground for human trafficking, but you would be wrong. Human trafficking exists in "good" and "bad" neighborhoods without such distinctions. In good neighborhoods you can find domestic servants working under circumstances equal to slavery and in those same neighborhoods you will find conventioneers and business travelers in $300-a-night hotel rooms seeking prostitutes online who are forced to work the trade by pimps and other elements of organized crime. In those bad neighborhoods you will find brothels buried deep inside ethnic communities offering underage boys and girls brought illegally to this country to be slaves for the sole purpose of sexually gratifying people from their own cultural group. Such brothels are almost impossible to root out due to the general fear police engender in many immigrants. In bad neighborhoods you might also find pimp-forced prostitution, a homegrown form of human trafficking. On these dark streets there you will find minor and adult prostitutes, both forced to sell their bodies by pimps who keep the money.

In both of these communities you will often find massage parlors and spas that cater exclusively to men. Most of these enterprises are nothing more than brothels offering a variety of sexual services for sale. There are also places where many women and children from other countries become sexual slaves and thus victims of human trafficking. Atlanta is home to many Asian massage parlors, which should not indict Asians; it should indict American society. If we had not created an economy where Asian women have become an exotic fetish rather than treasured individuals created in the image of a loving God, such locations would never even exist.

According to a report prepared for the US Central Intelligence Agency by Amy O'Neill Richard, an analyst with the State Department's Bureau of Intelligence and Research, Asian-organized crime made considerable gains in establishing its predominance in human trafficking women for use as sexual slaves during the 1990s. Most of the successes in Atlanta and around the United States took place unnoticed by local state and federal law enforcement.

In the report, Richard noted newly emerging hubs of entry for trafficked women: Atlanta, Cleveland, Houston, Orlando, and Washington-Dulles. She states, "Atlanta's airport was chosen as the main entry point for a Thai trafficker who brought 90 women into the city during 1994 and 1995. He selected Atlanta because the city was preparing for the Olympics at the time and he believed the Thai women would fit in well with the many ethnic nationalities that were arriving daily at the time. Additionally, Atlanta was an attractive city because of the low number of Asian ethnic immigration officials working there."[10]

As the 1990s drew to a close, the traffickers became even more brazen in their efforts to rule prostitution in the Atlanta area. During that time, an organized crime task force in Atlanta indicted 13 members of an Asian smuggling ring for trafficking up to 1,000 Asian women and girls, some as young as 13, to Atlanta and other US cities for prostitution. The women and girls were held in bondage until their $30,000 to $40,000 contracts were paid off. One brothel was described by law enforcement as a "prison compound" with barbed wire, fences, chained dogs, and gang members who served as guards.[11]

SPAS AND THE SEX TRADE

At the beginning of this chapter I referenced massage parlors and spas with their possible connections to organized crime. There are a number of Asian massage parlors near the intersection of Interstate 85 and Piedmont Avenue, along Cheshire Bridge Road and among the adjacent side streets. While I cannot state firsthand knowledge that these businesses are run by organized crime, I am able to state that police records show a number of these businesses rank among the most raided by law enforcement, netting more arrests than any other grouping of massage parlors in the city.

The Gold Spa on Piedmont is the center of the Asian massage parlor universe in Atlanta. Numerous men who claim to be patrons of the establishment have reviewed it online. These men hold back nothing when writing detailed reviews of the sexual services available there. In June 2009, the Gold Spa made national headlines when a security officer was shot a number of times in the chest in the back parking lot. He was pronounced dead upon arrival at Grady Hospital.

After many police raids, numerous arrests, and an escalation of crime in the general vicinity of the Gold Spa, perhaps the most notorious massage parlor in Georgia, *nothing* has changed. No local, state, or federal law enforcement agency and no city or county government have seen fit to enforce their "nuisance laws" to close the business. The Gold Spa stands as a symbol for everything wrong with Atlanta's attitude about prostitution and human trafficking dating back to the 1990s. Asian massage parlors and spas have operated in Atlanta with impunity for so long that to challenge them in any way brings a certain response.

Kelly Wright, a reporter from the FOX News Channel Washington bureau who was preparing a story on human trafficking, asked me to act as a tour guide with regard to underage prostitution, human trafficking, the political aspects of the issue, and what was being done in the way of rescue facilities. Not only had I just been doing similar research; I had also built alliances with many of the people he would want to interview for the program. Over two days I worked with Kelly as he pieced together a story that would feature State Senator Renee Unterman, Mary Frances Bowley of Wellspring Living (a local rescue facility for underage prostitutes), and

Bruce Ladebu who works to rescue child slaves internationally through his Child Rescue Initiative, along with Dillon.

On the morning of the final day, I was in the Buckhead area of Atlanta. Mr. Wright decided he wanted to interview Dillon and myself on Piedmont Avenue in front of Gold Spa, which is directly across the street from the Aroma Therapy Spa and the St. James Spa. We arrived on the area about 10:30 A.M. and parked our vehicles a block or so away from the shoot location. By 10:40 A.M. we were set up and the interviews began. Bruce Ladebu came along for the ride and brought his camera to record the event. Within five minutes of our arrival in front of the Gold Spa it was as though we had stepped on an anthill. Mamasans and working girls from every spa in the area were sticking their heads out of their front doors, furiously pointing while shouting into cell phones to unknown individuals. I got the distinct idea based on their body language that there were times when the women were speaking on the phone to one another from spa to spa to spa. Within ten minutes of our arrival a very menacing brown SUV sporting heavily tinted windows showed up in the parking lot of the Aroma Therapy Spa. The driver behind the partially lowered window was a man sporting sunglasses, a cell phone, and a lot of attitude. Before long someone in the vehicle was taking pictures and video of us.

The hunters had become the hunted.

You might think that when placed under the microscope, the people operating at the edge or beyond the edge of the law might recoil from publicity and hide. But those who profit from Asian massage parlors and the profits that they generate through prostitution and sometimes human trafficking are brazen. They are not afraid of law enforcement, politicians, prosecutors, reporters, or television cameras. But know this — they are very much afraid of you. When the citizens of Atlanta grow tired of sex trafficking and the international criminal organizations that make them possible, we can put an end to them.

PROFITING FROM PROSTITUTION

There are many people other than the pimps and traffickers who profit from massage parlors. There are the billboard companies who rent advertising space along the interstate, real estate companies who lease property in which the brothels are operated, and landowners who profit from the enterprise when they receive monthly lease payments. Some publications such as those mentioned in this chapter profit from the ads they sell in their adult services sections.

On behalf of my nonprofit organization Mercy Movement I recently undertook the task of wading through county tax records, the corporation division of the Georgia secretary of state, and used a number of other public legal means to discover the real estate owner of a building being leased by one of the most notorious and often raided Asian massage parlors on Piedmont Avenue in Atlanta. All my years of law enforcement should have prepared me for what I would find. I was expecting to find the property to be owned by some evil crime lord in a warehouse in a rundown section of town. Instead I discovered that the owner of the building was a real estate investor living in Buford, Georgia, a somewhat idyllic suburban community boasting the biggest mall in the Southeastern United States and a number of planned living communities that almost anyone would be excited to call home. It is a wonderful place to live, definitely not the seedy hideout of someone you would expect involved in Atlanta's most notorious sexual services operations.

So as this chapter draws to an end I write directly to this real estate owner on Piedmont Avenue and those like him. I now know where you are. I know what other enterprises you operate in your happy suburban environment even if those in your social circle of influence do not.

To everyone who profits in any way from prostitution and the human trafficking it creates, whether billboard companies, real estate companies, landowners, newspapers, and Internet companies, we are working to expose and end your involvement in modern-day slavery, starting right here in our hometown area of Atlanta.

CHAPTER 4

SLAVERY ON VACATION: ORLANDO, FLORIDA

C☆H☆A☆R☆L☆E☆S

IN THE SPRING of 2009, I visited the Youth with a Mission (YWAM) base in Orlando, Florida, to teach in one of their ongoing schools. During my first session I mentioned my work to fight human trafficking and sexual slavery. In the break between sessions, two of my students asked if I thought human trafficking was a problem in Orlando. My answer was yes. Certainly the problem is as local as it is global.

Their reply to me was, "Prove it."

Not being one to refuse a challenge, I answered, "I will."

SMALL TALK IN ORLANDO

Over the next five days I spent the free time during my afternoons and evenings using the Internet, local magazines, the Yellow Pages, and an assortment of investigative techniques and methods from prior investigative training to probe the issue. By the end of the week I had discovered more than 30 spas and massage parlors I strongly suspected to be employing foreign women likely trafficked into the United States for use as prostitutes. In almost every case in Orlando the business was clearly run by Asian-organized crime. How could I be sure? Even though I spotted a whole host of indicators for human trafficking, such as 24/7 service, firearms, or extreme security systems including bodyguards in some cases, one indicator stood out from among the rest. It was the consistent language barrier I discovered in each business. When you walk into a massage parlor or spa where not a single person in the building speaks English, and you repeat the process day after day, hour after hour, there is only one explanation: organized crime.

Most women wouldn't say, "I want to immigrate to America and become a prostitute" of their own free will. The criminal methods being employed are well established and easily spotted.

A criminal organization regularly brings what they call "fresh women" into the US to work its brothels in the big-city markets, replacing women who have had more time on the job. These more experienced and trusted prostitutes are then moved within their respective organizations or sold to others to work brothels along interstate highways across the United States or in smaller communities.

My investigative method was to enter the lobby of a suspected brothel posing as a tourist who had never previously visited such an establishment. I then asked questions about the services offered there, took a tour of the facilities, asked to meet all the girls working that day, and made general conversation for as long as possible to allow myself time to look for the signs of human trafficking-related prostitution. My goal was to not break a single law and not cause further harm to possible victims.

Sometimes I was invited back to one of the private rooms where I could further observe the operation. I continued making small talk with my assigned girl whenever possible. Yet most of the women I met could not understand a word I was saying. I would stay until I thoroughly frustrated the massage parlor madam, who would eventually demand that I go with a girl to her room and spend some money or leave the building. I always left, but not before I was able to determine with reasonable certainty whether or not to label the business a brothel staffed by illegally trafficked women. I immediately wrote and published a number of articles about my experiences across several national magazines and Web sites.

At the end of my week in Orlando I spoke to a gathering of all the students and teachers at YWAM Orlando and reported the findings of my weeklong investigation. As I expected, there were a few gasps, looks of shock, and whispers among those gathered. Young people — especially those committed to living out their faith at YWAM — really care about issues like human trafficking. They are the kind of people who are willing to uproot their lives and sell everything they own to change the lives of others, including in many of the hard places around the world. In the end we prayed for guidance on how each of us should proceed with this new knowledge.

It should be of interest to those readers who live in the Greater Orlando area that their local entertainment newspaper, *Orlando Weekly*, was a huge help to me in locating many of the Asian spas and massage parlors throughout the city that were part of my investigation. Those included many of the locations where women didn't speak English, who appeared to be living 24 hours a day at the establishment, and those in which I was propositioned by the staff, which offered sex for money. Yes, I believe in the freedom of the press and freedom of speech, but no legitimate press should allow itself to be used by criminals whose purpose is to steal the freedoms and dignity of others. I would urge every advertiser of the *Orlando Weekly* to stop placing ads in that publication until the owners stop accepting advertisements from massage parlors and spas.

ONE YEAR LATER

It was Friday and my time in Orlando was up for that week. After what I had discovered, I knew I would be back.

On my second trip a year later I tried to evaluate whether or not the problem had grown better or worse. During and following my third trip to Orlando later that same year, I sought to make contact with law enforcement officials to determine if they had encountered organized crime involvement in human trafficking and street level forced prostitution. Over several weeks I spoke with a number of people from the Orlando Police Department, the Orange County Sheriff's Department, the Kissimmee Police Department, and the Florida Department of Law Enforcement.

Repeatedly, none of them were willing to speak with me if the topic was human trafficking. The closest success I had was a spokesperson for the Orlando Police Department who remarked, "I think we had one case of human trafficking in Orlando a few years ago, but we referred it to the Florida Department of Law Enforcement."

"One case?" I replied. At least it was a start. Next, I called the Florida Department of Law Enforcement. Unfortunately a representative for the Florida Department of Law Enforcement Public Affairs appeared to clearly dodge my attempts to communicate, claiming, "Just keep calling. We'll eventually work something out, call back again next week." Nothing ever "worked out."

I wish I could report that contact with all of these vital law enforcement agencies yielded information about the work each of them is doing to fight human and sex trafficking and pimp-forced prostitution across central Florida, but they weren't talking.

At the time of this writing, they still aren't responding to contacts on this issue. I don't know if their lack of cooperation was due to departmental policy, political in nature, pressures brought to bear from the tourism industry, or simply understaffed offices and underconcerned leadership on the issue, but apparently questions about human trafficking near central Florida's vacation destinations run into a strange silence.

Since law enforcement contacts were not responsive, I turned to the community itself and found an expert on the problem who was more than willing to tell us about street-level forced prostitution in Orlando. I discovered her from an unlikely source. One day I was speaking with my publisher, Andrea Mullins, about my investigations in Orlando and corresponding frustrations. With her trademark encouraging voice she shared, "I have a friend in Orlando who works the streets to rescue women from street prostitution and pimps. Her name is Lynn Latham. You should give her a call."

COMPASSION IN ACTION

I'm glad I did. Lynn Latham is an incredible person of faith. She's an anomaly: a church lady with street credibility. Lynn is also a straight shooting, Bible-toting, hard-driving instrument of God's mercy and grace. In short, Lynn is compassion in action. She accomplishes on the streets what so many church services seek to accomplish. She is Jesus to people who will not meet Him without her presence in the tough places. If you haven't figured it out already, I highly admire Lynn. She's another one of those people whose walk with God I have a high regard for and desire to emulate.

On my next trip to Orlando, I brought my film crew to Lynn. What she shared that day has since become a primer for the many people who have asked me in the last two years, "How can I get involved in the fight against human trafficking and sex trafficking?" Following is some of the information we discussed in our interview conversation together. Though shortened and edited for clarity in print, Lynn's passion is so strong and her wisdom so insightful that I wanted to share as much of it as possible with you.

CP: Lynn, tell us who you are and tell us a little about your ministry before you got to Orlando. Then share what you've been doing in regard to women that you've been rescuing on the street.

LL: I started out in West Texas, ended up in California teaching school, went back to Texas for seminary, then moved to Virginia, and then Orlando and make that 32 years of ministry so far with the North American Mission Board (the national missions program of the Southern Baptist Convention). I came here thinking: "I could do everything;" But nobody here knew that, nobody here knew what a great person I was [laughs]. And so the first couple of months I had nothing to do. No church called me, no church wanted me to come teach them how to "do ministry." I had to do something on my own and so I went out driving, praying up and down the streets trying to see this area. This area was 34 little towns until Disney World came in and "Bam!" went the city. One is a beautiful city on top: it's called "the city beautiful," Orlando. But underneath it is a filthy, filthy, vile city that most people don't see and don't know about. God has equipped me through the years to learn lots of ways of working with people, accepting lots of different kinds of people, and realizing that Christianity is not that I'm a Baptist or that I'm a missionary, but that I am a follower of Christ and I'm going to tell His story to others.

CP: Tell us about this work of yours rescuing women from the streets.

LL: It kind of started out with the prayer driving. I saw the needs, I saw women standing on the corners begging, teenage kids begging. I thought they were begging for food but there were many other things they were begging for. Many were selling themselves, but I began giving them food and health kits. So it started out that way and then I just started praying, "Lord, send somebody to work with these people on the street." And I prayed and I prayed and I drove and I drove, and I'm still waiting for the churches to ask me to do my job.

But after work at night I was driving around looking and praying. One night I got upset with God. I just said, "God! Send a man down here to preach to these people!" And I heard this small voice that said, "I have." And I went, "You have what?!" It said, "I've sent someone." And I looked around and I didn't see anyone and I realized He was talking about me. And so I said, "OK, God, if You think I'm going to do this, *what* am I going to do?" And He said, "Look beyond the surface." And I looked beyond the people to the places behind them and I thought, "You know, I could go into those places." Well, you can imagine a gentleman's club, a strip club, a bar. A very conservative Baptist woman doesn't just walk in there and talk to them. So I kind of backed off, and I do that a lot, I step back and try and figure out what God wants me to do, not what I want. Because sometimes what I want and what He wants are not the same.

And so I backed off, and I continued to tell the pastors here and the people here and my friends around the states, and I've had so many because I've lived so many places, that I just needed prayer. Well, one friend told another friend who told another and a man from Texas called me, a pastor down in the valley, who was a police profiler, and he said, "I heard you want to go into the clubs. I'll come and teach you how," and I went, "I don't want to go into the clubs. I don't want to do it." He said, "I'll fly into Orlando and I'll teach you." So we went into a strip club, we paid the cover charge, and I'd say, "May I please speak to the manager?" And they'd say, "She's at the bar." So I'd go up to the bar and say, "Could I please speak to your girls?" And she'd say, "What for?" I said, "I just want to tell them about the best friend they could have." She'd say, "Get out." So we're doing this, we've gone through this several times and this one last time, and you know, it's been four hours, and kicked out of every club and I finally said, "Yeah, I'm ready to stop." And I get to the door and the bouncer stops us and says, "Why were you here?" I said, "We just wanted to tell them about the best friend they could have — Jesus." And he said, "They need that." And I stepped out into the night and I was brokenhearted. And I realized that God would not let me go. This was not what I wanted to do, I wanted to be married with a family and kids but there are so many women in this country that need someone to say, "You're special." And so I promised Him I'd do that.

CP: How do you rescue women from the pimp-forced prostitution? What's the danger there?

LL: Let me just tell you that none of this has anything to do with me. It's all a God thing. And God leads and God directs. I hear about women, I get phone calls about women and many of them want safety and we have a chance to help them. It's dangerous. There's usually somebody watching them all the time. And so you have to be careful. You have to meet people in a safe place. We use restaurants a lot, even the parking lot of a famous fast food restaurant . The women come and meet me and I tell them what I'm going to look like and what I'm wearing. And we get them out. There really was no place for them to go 14 years ago and that was a difficult thing. Then God finally opened a place called Restoration Ministries for Women where the women coming out of jail could live, work, get their lives back together, and contact their families. A place where inside themselves, they could make a choice that Jesus Christ was the answer. I can get them safe, but it's still up to them to decide what they want to do.

CP: What's probably the worst area in Orlando that you've worked in?

LL: I think the scary part to me was that particular part of town where the police wore black hoods. They were called the Dukes, so nobody would know who they were. So here I am driving around, white face, driving around with my car. I do a lot of driving around and checking out neighborhoods.

CP: Earlier you told me a little bit about some of the things that you've seen in Orlando. Let's talk about the Asian spas, the whole organized crime situation here in central Florida. What do you see in the spas in regard to human trafficking?

LL: Let me just tell you about one official one, that was two Christmases ago down on International Drive. Someone noticed that the girls who worked in the spa place were not leaving the building. And so they started watching, and they got the police watching, and they finally broke it up at

Christmas and there were ten women living upstairs who were not allowed to leave the building. Anytime someone holds your papers or coerces you to do something, that is trafficking. The women did massages and they were doing other things involved with "the massage industry."

CP: Are you seeing any other organized crime groups moving in from other parts of the world? In addition to the Asian spas, I've heard reports that some Eastern Europeans are involved.

LL: Absolutely. Russians (including former Soviet nations), the Thai have a large industry, and Asian Indians too. With regard to Hispanics, we have a lot of migrants who work on the farms who are held on the farms by chains and locks.

CP: Have you seen any of this yourself?

LL: I have. I was at the church and someone was sharing with me about a family member of theirs and they said, you need to take a drive down this country road, take a left and then a right. And so when I finished speaking, I did. I went down there and sure enough, I could see trailers back in there — *with families* — 10 or 15 Hispanic families — and the gates were locked and they could not leave on their own.

CP: Across the country we basically are finding that the church in America is peacefully coexisting with human trafficking, unaware of its presence. Any thoughts?

LL: I think it's more unawareness than anything. And I think when you ask me who's helping me with my work, church women are the ones helping me. Mainly in church it's the women who are becoming more aware of human trafficking and the women are reaching out.

CP: In these massage parlor situations I often discover that they are actually managed and run by women; I see a lot of exploitation of women by women. Why is that?

LL: Because that's where the money is.

CP: What advice do you give to people who want to help fight human trafficking?

LL: Number one: I'd advise them to start where I started and that's prayer. And number two is to drive around and see what's happening. Learn what's going on. Open your eyes. Most people are just not aware. A Christian's heart is full of love and compassion where the world is full of evil. So we're just completely different people and we haven't learned yet how to be tough. God wants us to be both tough and smart.

CP: Could you tell us about a particular girl you have rescued and her story? You don't have to use her name.

LL: I can tell you about a young woman I met. She had been prostituted in Indianapolis, Indiana. When I said, "Did you have a pimp?" she said, "Oh no, it was my boyfriend." And I said, "Well, did he try and prostitute you?" And she said, "Well, I never thought about it." But for years she had been on drugs and had been used. She had tried many times to get out and made some choices and finally did. And I had lunch with her this week and she said, "Today's my three-year anniversary of being clean and sober (and away from pimp prostitution)." And she said, "It's due to you, and to the Lord." And I said, "No, it's due to the Lord."

CP: That's awesome. Are any of these women ever beaten if they try to leave?

LL: I'm amazed at how brutal people are to each other and especially the women who put up with this. I had a friend, long-haired redhead, beautiful woman. And she was with a "boyfriend," actually a "John" (prostitution customer) who was being robbed. They killed him and then went after her. They beat her up and the next time I saw her she was in jail for murder, because they thought she was involved in his murder. Her hair was cut; her face was black and blue. Her arms were twisted; I've seen more women with their teeth knocked out just right in their face. We've paid for a lot of teeth to be fixed. But it's just an anger issue, there's a lot of anger, a lot of, "You didn't do what I told you" (from the pimps).

CP: So if they don't submit themselves to have sex with men for money, or do whatever their pimp says, they get beaten?

LL: Right. And at the same time the cops are saying, "If you'll lead us to them then we'll protect you." Then they lead them to the "John" and then they don't protect them and then they end up in jail. They're getting it from both sides.

That perfectly explains the plight of women caught up in pimp-forced prostitution and sexual slavery. They end up on the receiving end of problems from both pimps and law enforcement. These women are victims of violence, disease, addiction, poverty, and despair and get none of the money. My meeting with Lynn told me a lot about how everyday people can start making a difference in their own communities.

ARMED PIMPS

One day while working on the Orlando segment of our *Not in My Town* video, I was out with a film crew on Orlando's Orange Blossom Trail, or OBT, as the locals call it. We had just had a conversation about prostitutes and pimps carrying guns. I had told them that most prostitutes did not carry guns, but that you could be sure that no pimp is ever far away from a weapon of some sort. When I had made that statement I didn't know that in just minutes I would prove that theory true. We soon observed what appeared to be a street prostitute and her pimp who hovered nearby. We had seen several of them during my tour of the area for the video crew, but there was something a little different about this young woman. I was drawn to speak with her. I parked the van a safe distance from her in order to protect the film crew. I left the van in a parking lot about 50 yards behind where she stood on the street and approached her to learn about her situation.

Our encounter began this way.

"How's it goin'?"

I said this to the pimp who was sitting on a bus bench. His hand was gripping the black handle of an automatic pistol of some sort. I could see it protruding from a zippered pouch. I gave him no indication that I saw or was concerned about the gun. I just gave him one of those looks you give another guy on the streets meant to tell him I'm here and I'm neither worried about nor impressed by his presence.

Then I turned my attention directly to the young woman. She had dirty blond colored hair, dark blue jeans, and a pea green, low-cut blouse. A brown purse hung from her right shoulder.

She gave me no smile and not much encouragement. She just feverishly chewed her gum and waited for me to speak first. I was certainly not the first man to approach her that day, but she had her own rhythm, her own way of doing business, and it started with the man speaking first.

"Hey there, you look like you live here and I don't," I said.

"Yeah," she said.

"I'm trying to get to Medieval Times and I've been lost the whole time I've been in this town."

There is no way in the world that I can ever learn about the inner workings of life on the streets if I walk up to pimps and prostitutes and tell them I'm doing research or investigating human trafficking and ask them to play 20 questions. Being undercover means a cover story about who I am and what I'm doing there is a must. I'm not arguing theology at this point; I'm trying to help change a life.

"Medieval Times. Well, actually I moved here from Texas," she shared.

"From Texas? No way! I used to live in Houston. What about you?"

"I lived in Austin," she said.

"Austin, cool. What are you doing here now?" I asked.

"Just working," she answered hesitantly. "Are you visiting?"

"Yeah, just visiting. I'm a tourist," I continued.

"OK, cool. Is that your van over there?" she said.

"Yeah."

"Do you have a hotel nearby?"

I played dumb at this point. "Do I have a hotel near here? Yeah, I'm staying just down the street."

"Well, I'm not Medieval Times, but I do take cash," she offered.

Let me be clear: I will not under any circumstances ever break the law doing research or in the course of an investigation. I will not incriminate myself ever for any reason. In this case, I started the conversation and answered questions.

At this point, she had, in many jurisdictions, incriminated herself. In fact, if she had been an undercover police officer she would have been guilty of entrapment in many jurisdictions by inferring that she could be bought for money. I looked back over my shoulder at the bus stop bench where her pimp sat leering at me, his hand still holding the grips of his black automatic pistol. Time to flee.

"You what?" I said.

"I do take cash . . . or wine," she repeated.

"Or wine?" Never heard that one before.

"Yes, wine or cash."

"Oh, I just caught on to what you are talking about."

I am undercover so I cannot say why I am really there speaking with her. In reality I am there to find out how a woman gets to this lowly place. Why would she sell herself to strangers and then give all the money to someone else? What is in the mind of a pimp? I am there to answer dozens of questions through observation and I only have between one and two minutes per encounter on the streets to get some answers. What I am doing is dangerous whether I come in contact with pimps and prostitutes or undercover cops, none of whom want journalists and writers interfering with the work they are there on the streets to perform. I am there to learn to help keep other girls like this one from falling into the same trap.

Preparing to turn and leave, this young girl extends the conversation. "I'm out here working so . . ."

"You're working?" I stop, taking a chance I usually don't. "Do you work by yourself or for someone else?"

"Um, I work for myself," she answered, as her eyes passed my left shoulder to connect with her impatient pimp.

"How long have you been doing this? Have you ever had any trouble?"

"Sometimes . . . not much."

"Isn't it dangerous out here?"

"It is, but I gotta do what I gotta do, you know?"

"Have you done this very long?"

"A couple of months maybe? I just started. I just moved here. I've got tons of stuff to pay for."

"What made you decide to do this?"

"Are you looking for something? If not I gotta move on."

I made it clear I was not "looking for something" and that I would be leaving. Before I left, I introduced myself as Chuck and extended my hand to shake hers. She said her name was Megan.

TWO MEGANS

That's when I knew why God wanted me to stop and speak with this particular girl. I repeated her name — "Megan" — as I was shaking her hand, quickly turning to return to the safety of my van.

Ironically, my own daughter, also named Megan, was seated in the van with our camera crew not 50 yards away from where I was standing. She even shared a few things in common with "Street Megan."

My daughter Megan was from Texas just like "Street Megan."

My daughter Megan is in her mid-20s just like "Street Megan."

My daughter Megan has hair about the same color as "Street Megan's."

My daughter Megan was a good conversationalist just like "Street Megan."

But there were a few differences as well.

My daughter Megan would be spending the night in the safety of her own hotel room; "Street Megan" would be forced by her pimp to share a number of hotel rooms, having sex with strangers and fearing whether she would live to see another day.

My daughter Megan had worked her way through the University of Georgia earning a degree in International Affairs and Public Policy and was now working on her second degree in business from a small Christian college. In contrast "Street Megan" was working her way to the bottom as fast as she could get there.

My daughter Megan's future choices include freedom, opportunity, and likely increased levels of success. "Street Megan," if following statistics for her line of work, will likely die within the next seven years due to violence, drugs, or a sexually transmitted disease.

My daughter has me in her life, a mother, and other family and friends for support. While "Street Megan" has a strong male figure in her life, his purpose is different. His goal is to make money regardless of what happens to Megan, whether rape, abuse, disease, or death. She is not free to leave. She is not free to live as she pleases. She is in every aspect of the definition, a modern-day slave.

When I got back in the van I told everyone to be quiet and stay down. Then I told them that the pimp sitting at the bus stop was holding a gun. Next, I made eye contact in the rearview mirror with my daughter sitting in back of the van.

I looked at her for a long time. My Megan, my daughter, was safe. Yet I continued to think about "Street Megan" as I drove away. She was someone's daughter too, with a father and mother who disappeared at some point along the way. She needed someone to help, to show mercy, to stand up for that other someone's daughter.

Whether they are pimp-forced prostitutes, kidnapped in the US and then trafficked across the country, or women from other countries brought into the here as sex slaves, they are all somebody's daughters.

Even if they are no longer loved by someone where they once called home, they are still God's children and that makes them my sisters and my responsibility. They are our sisters and daughters. Now that you know, there is no option but to do something about it.

CHAPTER 5

WHAT HAPPENS IN VEGAS . . .

C☆H☆A☆R☆L☆E☆S

BY NOW, MY year of prayer, study, and investigation of human trafficking and sexual slavery in the United States was well under way and my travels extended westward.

It was a perfect evening.

I had just finished a weekend of speaking engagements in northern California, one of my favorite places on earth. Thanks to a ride from a friend I made it to the airport early enough to get a bite to eat before boarding my flight from Fresno to Las Vegas. I had specifically chosen this time of day, my favorite time of day to fly, early evening just before sundown.

After a brief flight I would be landing at McCarran International Airport as the lights on the Las Vegas Strip turned on, almost as if they'd been lit in honor of my arrival.

Now before you stop reading long enough to ask, "Hey, why are you talking so highly about the virtues of Las Vegas?" allow me to explain that I was traveling to Las Vegas to interview Craig Gross, founder of Fireproof Ministries and XXXchurch.com, an organization dedicated to helping those connected with the porn industry or addicted to porn to find a way out through the love of Christ. I was to interview Craig about his work and get his take on prostitution and human trafficking in Vegas and throughout Nevada. As for my praise of the lights on the Strip, I will make no apologies. I was born in a small town, so I love the lights of the big city. There is an undeniable excitement and electricity that makes the city part of the attraction it has become.

NO CLOUDS IN SIGHT

But back to the flight. According to some experts, takeoffs are statistically the most dangerous time in any flight followed closely by landings. The actual time in flight is the safest time of all. So I figured that I would simply pray hard and endure the first five minutes after takeoff, relax for a while, and then by the time I was ready to get nervous about the landing we'd already be safely on the ground. No problem, right?

The plane took off without incident (my prayers had been answered!) and in minutes we are were cruising toward our destination through azure blue skies without a cloud in sight, having just been promised that any minute the flight crew would be passing down the aisles ready to offer my favorite plane beverage, ginger ale over crushed ice. It really felt good to be alive.

A few moments later, there was a sudden, loud popping noise, then a loud bang followed by the sounds of tearing metal coming from the rear of the fuselage in the approximate location of the right rear engine. The aircraft began shaking violently, then banked to the left and angled slightly downward.

I quickly turned to the lady sitting across the aisle with her young baby and said, "That didn't sound good!" Then I shamelessly started praying fervently *out loud* in every form I could muster: "God, please don't let me die . . . my family needs me so much."

That was my mantra. "God, please don't let me die . . . my family needs me so much. God, please don't let me die . . . my family needs me so much."

Before I could repeat the phrase a fourth time, the smell of acrid smoke shot through the cabin. The lady next to me lost it completely. She began sobbing and clutched her child tightly, whispering her own mantra: "God, please don't let my baby die. God, please don't let my baby die. God, please don't let my baby die."

Simultaneously, each passenger responded to the event in his or her own way. Some prayed. Some cried. Others hyperventilated. People turned on their cell phones against FFA policy to call loved ones, shouting there had been an explosion in the rear of the plane and they weren't sure if they would make it. The moment grew worse for everyone onboard when the pilot came on the intercom. Usually pilots underplay every bad situation in an effort to bring calm to the passengers. For our pilot, that moment had passed.

"Ladies and gentlemen, we have suffered a catastrophic engine failure. I am attempting to get us back to the airport in Fresno, but we are losing altitude every few miles and we may be forced down somewhere between our current position and the airport. Flight crew, prepare the cabin for an emergency landing."

Every word of potential doom the pilot spoke to us was punctuated by cacophonous bells, alarms, and warning signals which urged him to get off the intercom and get back to the job of fighting with the plane for our survival. But the alarms and bells didn't make me nearly as afraid as the fear I heard in the pilot's voice. Apparently I wasn't the only one to sense it. The flight attendants started crying while running in all directions. The pilot then slowly and skillfully turned our badly damaged plane back toward Fresno.

The quiet guy next to me turned and laughed in stoic fashion. "You want to know what's funny? I've spent my entire adult life as a skydiving instructor without ever experiencing a single mishap. Now I'm on a plane that could crash and I'm sitting here without a parachute." Then he shook his head as if to put some distant regret back into its cage and stared out the window blankly. In the silence he had imposed I realized he had not really been talking to me. Instead, his statement was more a final act of contrition than anything else as he sat quietly awaiting his fate.

About a minute after our pilot made his successful turn toward Fresno, the plane shook violently again and dropped straight down about 100 feet. Screams and prayers escalated in the chaos. Again and again the plane dropped, robbing us of precious altitude we could not hope to regain as minutes and miles took forever to accomplish their end. Then after everyone involved was physically and emotionally drained, the pilot announced that the airport was in sight and we had been cleared for an immediate emergency landing. With very little fanfare our ordeal ended. We were safely on the ground.

Since this incident I have looked into the important physical factors regarding this flight. Based on our original flight altitude, an expert told me that if we had tumbled from the sky to the ground starting from the moment that the engine blew, it would have taken us between 45 seconds and 1 minute 15 seconds to impact the ground and then it would have all been over in an instant. *Around one minute of terror and then the end.* While I am grateful that was not our fate, the philosopher in me observed my own thoughts and feelings along with those of my fellow passengers during our dangerous flight back to Fresno. Every few miles we flew would be followed by the plane shaking and falling another hundred feet or more straight down without the ability to regain any altitude. Simple math told everyone on the plane that eventually we might run out of altitude before we made it back to a safe landing. What if we survived drop after drop and the initial event itself only to crash and die within sight if the airport?

It would have taken us at least 25 minutes to get back to the airport in Fresno. Twenty-five minutes to think about dying at any moment. Would the smoke return and choke us to death? Where there is smoke there is fire. Would a fire set off the fuel tanks and make our end a fireball in the sky? Forty-five seconds of terror might be a more humane end than 25 minutes of waiting for death with every passing second.

I trust God. I have been cut, shot, and have fought for my life on several occasions, but a near-death experience was a new one for me. I trust God, but after landing back in Fresno, I took it as God's will I needed to rent a car to make it for my meeting in Vegas.

DRIVING TO VEGAS

Instead of sunset, I arrived near sunrise around 5:30 A.M. the next morning. My hotel was at the so-called family-friendly Treasure Island where I checked in and slept for a couple of hours. The sleep was the fitful sleep of a man who'd had a brush with death followed by an all-night drive through the desert. By 9:00 A.M. I was awake again and waiting for Craig Gross.

I was glad I was interviewing a minister, because before we started the interview I used the opportunity to unburden myself to him about my harrowing experience the previous evening. By the time our breakfast arrived we had switched to the interview.

I've shared some of it below, simply with the desire to help you understand the issue from someone who serves those in trafficking situations in the one state in the US that includes 13 counties with legalized prostitution.

CP: Why did you move your ministry to Las Vegas?

CG: We had been coming to Las Vegas the last seven years ministering to people who attend porn conventions. Not a lot of porn is made in Las Vegas, but here is where it is all on display. The thought was, what kind of impact could we have on a day-to-day basis within this town. We wanted to expand XXXchurch.com from being more than just a ministry Web site to see if we could help people.

CP: Is it true that "what happens in Vegas stays in Vegas"?

CG: That's just not the case; that whole slogan is just a joke! There are 17 billboards around town that say, "Need to stay in Vegas one more night? Earn $500.00!" When you call the number, they tell you that they will give you the money if you will pose naked or masturbate on camera, but that's never going to get off the Internet. What we've seen is people making decisions while they are in town that will affect the rest of their lives, impact their marriage, and their relationship with the Lord. This isn't a place where you can just check out on your life back at home. Yet many people believe that and do things in this town that they would never do anywhere else. What we do is "intervention evangelism." If we can stand in the way of some of those things, if we could use the distractions in town to have a conversation with these people, that's what we want to do — to intervene *before* people make bad choices.

CP: What does XXXchurch.com do to help people with porn addictions?

CG: The Web site has become quite a large resource. We have the prayer wall where people can get connected. There is a section on the site for men, women, teens, spouses, and couples either addicted to or affected by porn. If we've left anyone out let me know! It's not just a guy's site. What do you do for a spouse who lost her husband to porn? Every Sunday when we speak somewhere I am approached by some woman in tears who tells me that (the sin of) porn is why she is divorced, so we have a section on the site for them. We have a free software called X3 Watch which monitors where you go online and sends a report about any questionable site that you look at to friend, a parent, a pastor or an accountability partner. We have a 30-day online workshop called "X3 Pure" that we just started as well because a lot of people do not want a counselor and will not join a small group, although I would recommend both of those things. By the fourth lesson we have hopefully made it clear to the individual that you can't do this on your own, because the end-all solution isn't you staring at a computer screen watching something. We are always adding to the resources available on our site.

CP: Tell me about your ministry in Nevada's legal brothels.

CG: There are 17 brothels in the state of Nevada, most in some of the smaller cities. The closest one is about 45 miles from Vegas and you can get there on a free shuttle from The Strip. We have connections at two of them. I started out by showing up at the door of one of these brothels and I apologized for how church people had acted toward them in the past. Everything we are doing here in Las Vegas is less about building a church and more about being the church. How can we serve people on the Strip or how can we serve these (brothel) gals? Our ministry to all these people comes with no strings attached. Even in the legal brothels, these girls live there and they work there and they can't leave during the weeks or months they are working the brothel. So the brothel owners care about making the girls happy and they are glad for our ladies to come in and spend time with them, doing their hair or nails, cooking for them, and shopping for them.

CP: Talk to me about street prostitution in Las Vegas.

CG: Vegas will tell you that prostitution is illegal in Clark County, but you do have some street prostitutes and there are some ministries that reach out to them. But you wouldn't see these women working the Las Vegas Strip, that is going on right out in the open. What you will see are billboards on the roadside and on the back of trucks that advertise, "Girls direct to your hotel room in 20 minutes or less!" Somehow they get away with calling that escorts or entertainment, but it's prostitution and they'll let you know it is "full service," which means sex as soon as you call their telephone number.

★ ★ ★ ★ ★

In Clark County, Nevada (includes Las Vegas), an entire court docket is scheduled one day each week to hear the cases of juveniles charged with prostitution; in 20 months, 226 juveniles from across the country were adjudicated by the court for prostitution/ prostitution-related offenses committed in Las Vegas. In the first half of 2007, 12.8% of the females committed to Caliente Youth Center had been adjudicated for the offense of solicitation for prostitution, a misdemeanor offense.[1]

ON THE STRIP

"The unexamined and unchallenged life is not worth living. What is needed most by some individuals to truly feel alive is a close brush with death."

While the sentiment is attributed occasionally to both Plato and Socrates, regardless of its origin, I have always thought it most perfectly described my approach to life. Craig gave me a lot of useful information about the dangers of Sin City, but I needed to go deeper if I was going to find actual evidence of human trafficking. First I got a few hours of much needed sleep. Then in the early evening I made my way out to the Strip feeling more alive than I had felt in some time. My experience on the plane had taken care of any fear or hesitation I had. I was ready to hit the streets of Las Vegas and find the evidence of human trafficking that I could sense was lurking just under the surface of the city.

For the second day in a row it was a perfect evening. Not too hot and absolutely no humidity. To use the poker vernacular of Las Vegas, a guy from the South will always, "See your Western dry heat, raise you Southern humidity, and win the hand every time."

I am a student of several diverse disciplines. These include behavioral science, creative writing, and law. I had been told that there were people who walked the sidewalks of the city with signs and business cards to advertise escorts to your room in 20 minutes or less. Monday night when I walked on the Strip, my behavioral science side kicked in. I determined to try an experiment. Not exactly scientific, but I did include some variables. I would walk the three blocks from my hotel, the Treasure Island Hotel and Casino, to the Bellagio Hotel, made famous in the film *Ocean's Eleven*. During my walk between the two hotels I would not ask for or seek any information on escorts, but if offered promotional materials for such from individuals or newspaper racks I would accept them. Those were my rules and I followed them.

The results were unnerving. The streets were lined with "card snappers," named for their technique of snapping escort collector cards between their fingers to get your attention. When you look their way they will hand you a couple of cards featuring one escort per card, often photographed nude, advertising that the girl in question is available for your entertainment pleasure in 20 minutes or less. In three blocks of walking I was offered more than 120 cards. On the public sidewalk I encountered a large newspaper rack that contained more than 20 different newspapers, each promoting numerous escort services and ads for individual escorts.

By the time I reached the Bellagio my pockets were full of filth, but my work was only beginning. I made my way back to the only quiet place I could find, my hotel room, where I started calling telephone numbers on the escort cards to ask if the girl on the card was available. Upon every single inquiry the operator told me the girl I asked for was busy, but it just so happened that she had another girl available who could be at my hotel room door in 10 to 20 minutes.

Most of the time, the substitute woman offered to me was described as exotic, Asian, new to the US, European, someone who speaks very little English, or something similar. Now I was getting closer to finding human trafficking. There were too many instances of bait and switch going on where the American girl on the advertisement was switched to a foreign woman. Then I discovered something else I hadn't considered until that moment. It took me about 30 minutes to walk from the Bellagio Hotel back to the Treasure Island and car traffic was gridlocked, even at night. It takes forever to get anywhere by car in Vegas. That meant only one thing. If the escorts can get to your hotel room in 10 to 20 minutes *they are already in or next to the hotel*. Girls are stationed at many hotels on the Strip waiting in bars, casinos, and hotel rooms for a call to send them to a room somewhere in the hotel where they are waiting.

Just imagine the level of criminal organization required to keep such an enterprise in operation 24 hours a day, 365 days a year. Imagine the profits that would be made by this organization if they used slaves as escorts. Women imported illegally from foreign countries sold on an auction block to the highest bidder, forced to work as prostitutes, inches away from the American Dream and yet a million miles away from it. The calls I made inquiring about the ads in the newspapers from earlier in the evening sometimes yielded the same results. I was occasionally offered foreign women instead of the Americans who were advertised and the operators were selling them as hard as they could. I also wondered how many of the women in the ads, regardless of nationality, were working in forced prostitution by a pimp, or as the women often call them, their "boyfriend."

By late Monday night I was suffering from overexposure to the dark spiritual forces that inhabit human trafficking and prostitution. Investigating such evil from the inside is like sticking your head into a toilet for hours at a time. Researching these crimes against the innocent takes a great toll on me as I operate in an atmosphere filled with total depravity. The worst part is that I am unable to bring immediate help to the victims I encounter. Beside the effects of Sin City, I hit a wall of physical fatigue and emotional drain that I was still feeling from my emergency landing coupled with an overwhelming need for restful sleep. As my head hit my pillow I determined to spend the following morning investigating spas and massage parlors in and around Las Vegas before heading to the airport for a less-eventful flight to Nashville, Tennessee.

BY THE POOL

That next morning I was up early, filled with a renewed sense of purpose. I quickly dressed and jogged downstairs in search of a good breakfast spot. In the process, I walked through a casino. In Vegas you can't get much of anywhere without being forced by the geography of the place to walk through a jungle of slot machines. I decided to have breakfast at the Kahunaville Tropical Restaurant on the patio near the pool. The air was dry, but overall the weather was sunny and pleasant. I found a table next to the water, ordered my breakfast, settled in, and mentally prepared for the day ahead of me.

It was 8:00 A.M. and the place was stacked with people who were either seeking their "place in the sun" or a good case of skin cancer, I'm not exactly sure. As I waited, I observed two young women who stood out, one blonde and one brunette. They appeared to be there for another day on the job, nothing special. It was obvious that they were *at* the pool, but not enjoying the day like everyone else.

They were waiting for an inevitable and completely expected interruption. Just after my food arrived, the signal came. The dark brunette received a call on her cell, immediately excused herself from her friend, and packed up her gear. She walked in my direction and stopped on the other side of a rail near my table. Apparently Miss Brunette must have thought that she was speaking in code that no one else could understand, but when she started talking she turned my suspicions about her activities from likely to definite. Her phone conversation went something like this:

> "Yeah, it's me. I was sitting near some people and I had to get away from them to answer."
>
> "Look, Mike, we got here on time and it's too early in the morning to be giving me any crap."
>
> "All right, all right! Just give me the guy's room number. . . . OK. Got it."
>
> "No, I can be up there in about ten minutes."
>
> "Got it. . . . He wants an hour and he says his name is Robert."
>
> "I'll call you after."

Then she walked away.

My brain spun full speed in undercover cop mode throughout her entire conversation until she spoke those final words, "I'll call you after." That's when the joy of investigating left me.

That's when she became someone's daughter.

That's when I was unable to eat my breakfast. That's when I had a problem. While I was searching throughout Las Vegas, Nevada, for evidence of human trafficking, I was aware many women choose prostitution as a profession of their own free will without any threats or force from anyone else. But that didn't stop my heart from breaking as the young woman with the brunette hair made her way to a room that could have been down the hall from mine to have sex with a stranger and did so under no visible coercion.

I sat there for a long time, ashamed to be a man, upset that *any* man could be so dehumanizing as to hand over money for a few moments of sexual gratification. Why? Because what happens in Vegas stays in Vegas, right? Or least that's the lie that is accepted to make the crime more palatable to those involved.

THE PERFECT CABBIE

I was still a little sick to my stomach around 10:00 A.M. when I hailed a cab just outside my hotel. I was fortunate for two reasons. First, my cabbie was a talker. Second, I didn't need a foreign language class for us to communicate. I got in and said, "Just drive."

We pulled away from the hotel and out onto the strip into surprisingly light traffic. I asked him to roll down the windows and the breeze on my face made my stomach a little less sour. After a couple of blocks the cabbie and I exchanged glances back and forth a few times in the rearview mirror, him wearing Ray-Ban Aviators and me wearing Harvé Benard sunglasses. Then he smiled at me and spoke, revealing a bit of accent from somewhere in the Caribbean.

"Where do you want to go, man? What you lookin' for? I know you don't just be lookin' for a ride."

Jackpot . . . the perfect cab driver. Direct and to the point. Offering to find me whatever vice I was seeking. My last day of investigation in Vegas, I chose to see where this guide could take me in furthering evidence of potential trafficking. "Take me to the part of town where a man can find women from other countries to party with," I said.

His response? "No problem, man. I know just where to go."

I soon saw this cab ride wasn't going to cost me very much money. In just a few minutes we made our way over to Spring Mountain Road where, in an area of about ten blocks, I counted more than 20 spas and massage parlors.

The cabbie asked, "Just pick one out and I'll stop the car."

I told him, "Why don't you just give me a tour of all the spas in the area. I might rent a car and come back later in the day."

"Oh, you must be just shoppin', man," he said.

If he only knew why I was really here, I thought.

Then he gave me a thorough tour of spas and massage parlors in Las Vegas. While none of them were located on the Strip they seemed to encircle it. Our tour took us from Spring Mountain Road to Decatur Boulevard to Sahara Avenue to Jones Boulevard to Flamingo Road to Paradise Road to Arville Street to Industrial Road until I began losing count of the streets where prostitution was both available and known to my cab driver.

As the meter fare climbed he eventually spoke again, "These places all get new women regularly. They come and then in a while they go and new women show up."

I said nothing, hoping he would say more.

"I bring regular customers out here all the time, men who are in and out of Vegas regularly. They always get what they are looking for and they always have new women to choose from."

THE XYZ SPA

Everything he had just told me amounted to good potential as evidence that human trafficking and organized crime were involved in the spas in Las Vegas. It takes a significant organization across several states to keep that many women on the move on a regular rotation. I told my driver to take me to the spa that was most frequented by his regular customers and he drove me to a spa I have renamed XYZ Spa for this writing. The driver waited as I walked inside.

The XYZ Spa was like many I had visited in Orlando. Upon entering I encountered Asian decor and a Buddhist shrine of some sort, but what was missing in the lobby was an ATM machine that many spas and massage parlors have installed to keep customers from having to leave to go get more "tip" money. I was greeted by a cordial Asian mamasan (who spoke very little English) and was led to a small room complete with bed and table with various oils. She asked me how long I wanted to stay, but I asked to see a lineup, which is a way of asking to see all of the women on duty. This was also my way of seeing the ages and conditions of the women at the spa. I use this ploy to stay in the establishment as long as possible, making observations before the mamasan demands that I buy time with one of the women or leave. There were four women available that day. One by one she had them come to the room and introduce themselves to me. As each of them entered the room I asked them simple questions to gauge their language ability and other factors.

I said, "Hi, my name is _____ . What's your name?" Each girl answered with a name and that's when I flipped the script on them.

"I'm from _____ . Where are you from?" In every case at the XYZ Spa, none of the women knew enough English to be able to answer my question.

"What time is it? Do you like my shirt?" On and on I continued, quickly learning that not one girl could carry a simple conversation in English. Again, this is not wrong, but points out that these girls had not likely been in the country long and were clearly not raised in an American, English-speaking culture.

How is the XYZ Spa operating a legitimate spa when these women didn't speak enough English to answer simple questions, much less pass state-mandated requirements for licensure as a massage therapist? It was clear they did not intend to provide massage services but that the location served as a front for brothel prostitution using women who were probably immigrated illegally or on short-term visas from Southeast Asia, likely China or South Korea.

Soon the mamsan returned. In her broken English, she gestured, "You choose now. You choose girl. Which girl you choose?"

I had pushed the limit as far as I could. "I might come back later. No girl right now."

"You no leave. You stay choose girl. Pretty girls. You really like massage good. You no leave. Stay."

I kept walking. She followed me to the door and nearly to my cab.

"That didn't take long," said my driver.

"I wasn't buying," I said. "Just looking. Take me back to my hotel."

He simply shook his head and drove me back to the Strip.

LEAVING LAS VEGAS

Later that afternoon I took another short cab ride, this time to McCarran International Airport. As I sat waiting for my flight, I reflected on my stay. I had been on the ground in Sin City no more than 30 hours. In that short time I had accomplished my goal of seeking evidence of human trafficking in Las Vegas. No, I didn't find "smoking gun" evidence of human trafficking in the city and I didn't rescue anyone from slavery, but I did find substantial support for my belief that organized criminal elements are behind much of the prostitution throughout the area. Sometimes my job is not rescue; sometimes it is investigation. Though my soul longs to do more, rescue will have to wait.

I was overwhelmed with everything I had learned and it was good to meet Craig Gross and hear about the good work he and his team are accomplishing in Vegas. I was pondering my interview with Craig when my flight was called. Just a few hours earlier I had been on a plane that had blown an engine in flight and almost crashed in the process. Now I had to get on a plane to Dallas and then another flight to Nashville to meet my video crew for a shoot there.

By the time I was able to will myself out of my seat in the terminal the plane was almost completely loaded and nearing last call. I took a deep breath and stood up. Then I took another deep breath and trusted God with my present and my future.

I have faced death many times in car accidents, in firefights with bullets flying past my head, through hurricanes, in a deadly fire in a high-rise building, and in third-world jungles and deserts. Any of these could have been my end, but God continues to have other plans for my life. It has been rightly said the safest place in the world is the center of God's will. God was leading me on this strange odyssey of discovery regarding human trafficking in America and I knew He wasn't finished with me yet.

I maneuvered onto the plane, settled into my seat, whispered a heartfelt prayer, then closed my eyes and rested.

For the first time in two days I really rested.

In an atmosphere where my mind should have generated fear, I found peace. God is like that. In the place where fears are born, God brings us peace.

The odyssey continued.

CHAPTER 6:

CALIFORNICATION: THE WORST (AND BEST) OF AMERICA'S NEW SLAVERY

D★I★L★L★O★N

> The problem of human trafficking has reached into neighborhoods throughout California and is one of the fastest growing criminal enterprises in the world. Individuals are bought, sold, transported and held in inhumane conditions for use in prostitution or as forced laborers. It would be morally and socially irresponsible to ignore this problem and the victims it creates in California every year.
>
> — SALLY LIEBER, California Assembly Member,
> September 21, 2005, at the signing of AB 22[1]

IN THE DOCUMENTARY *Dreams Die Hard*,[2] viewers are given a front-row view of a group of Mexican teenage girls who are provided safe travel across the California border. While some might think this passage would mark a point of freedom for a young person seeking a better life in a new country, the exact opposite is true. Within minutes, deals are arranged by the traffickers with day laborers seeking a quick thrill in the early afternoon. Money is exchanged. A deal is made.

Sex has been purchased and performed in broad daylight on American soil.

As disturbing as this sounds, the law enforcement officials performing surveillance say no rescue will take place today. Why not? A lookout is watching for people who may seek to intervene. In the case of a problem, the law enforcement team fears the girls and their traffickers would disappear before a rescue could be made. "It's all about losing the girls," the unit leader says. Their priority is to wait for a time when these girls can be rescued, not just forced to flee.

Unfortunately, far too many girls are being lost altogether in the process. As Kevin Bales, president of Free the Slaves, shares, "Even one slave is too many."[3] Yet thousands of trafficking victims pass through California. This includes not only sex trafficking victims, but other forms of forced labor, making it, according to some reports, the state with the nation's highest numbers for human trafficking (and certainly in the top three states, alongside Texas and Florida).

As I researched the latest news of trafficking cases in the San Diego region, I ran across what a district judge called one of the top five most serious cases prosecuted in sentencing a man in a July 2010 sex trafficking case. Adrian Zitlalpopoca-Hernandez, 33, had two teenage girls smuggled from Mexico to work as prostitutes in migrant camps over a several month period in 2008. He was sentenced to more than 24 years in federal prison. Such cases have increased in recent years in California, due to increases in criminal activity, legislation available to apply toward such cases, and awareness of the issue in the state.[4]

THE GOLDEN STATE: PRIME TARGET

Southern California, with its shared border with Mexico, international airport at LAX, and major port along the Pacific Coast, creates the perfect mix for traffickers seeking a transit point of operations. A California government report notes, "The state's extensive international border, its major harbors and airports, its powerful economy and accelerating population, its large immigrant population and its industries make it a prime target for traffickers."[5]

According to the Los Angeles-based Coalition to Abolish Slavery & Trafficking (CAST), Los Angeles is "one of the top three points of entry into this country for victims of slavery and trafficking. The diverse communities of this sprawling city make it easier to hide and move victims from place to place, making it very difficult for law enforcement to locate potential survivors."[6] Further, the organization asserts that, "immigration agents estimate that 10,000 women are being held in Los Angeles's underground brothels; his does not include the thousands of victims in domestic work, sweatshops, or other informal industries."[7]

To be clear, sex trafficking of Mexican immigrants is only one of many types of trafficking the state of California faces. In its report on the state of human trafficking in California, the following cases of note were mentioned from the past decade:

- *In December 2006, a financial settlement was reached on behalf of 48 Thai welders hired through Kota Manpower Inc. of Thailand and Los Angeles, accused of forcing them to live in squalor while working for little or no pay.*

- *In June 2006, a couple from Egypt pleaded guilty to forcing a 10-year-old Egyptian girl to work as a domestic servant to their family of seven in Irvine. The couple had forced the girl to sleep in the garage, with no light or ventilation, and had forbidden her to attend school or see a doctor in two years.*

- *In July 2005, the federal government arrested more than 40 people in Los Angeles and San Francisco and seized more than $3 million in illicit proceeds in Operation Gilded Cage. This operation involved more than 100 Korean women, many of whom told investigators that they were taken from their country against their will and forced to work as erotic masseuses.*

- *In September 2004, a financial settlement was reached on behalf of Nena Jimeno Ruiz, who was lured to Los Angeles from the Philippines under false pretenses, then forced to work 18-hour days at the home of an executive at Sony Pictures. She had to sleep on a dog bed and was threatened with never seeing her family again if she complained.*

- *In 2001, a Berkeley landlord and restaurateur, Lakireddy Bali Reddy, was sentenced to more than eight years in federal prison for smuggling teenage girls from India in a sex and labor exploitation ring spanning 15 years and operating in India and California. He repeatedly raped and sexually abused his victims and forced them to work in his businesses. A 17-year-old girl died of carbon monoxide poisoning in an apartment he owned.[8]*

NEW LAWS BRING PROGRESS

On the positive side, California has responded with the most extensive and comprehensive collaboration of legal initiatives, rescue and restore groups, and other anti-trafficking coalitions of any state in the nation. On the policy side, a wide variety of legislation has been put into law, some of which has become model legislation for other states. Most recently, former Governor Schwarzenegger signed Chelsea's Law, a new measure that sentences anyone convicted of certain sex offenses against a child to life in prison without parole. The law was named after 17-year-old Chelsea King, who was murdered in 2010 by a registered sex offender.[9] The bill, AB 1844, includes the following text regarding its heightened punishments specifically for domestic minor sex trafficking:

> *Under existing law, any person who deprives or violates the personal liberty of another with the intent to effect or maintain a felony violation of specified sex crimes, extortion, or to obtain forced labor or services, is guilty of human trafficking. Existing law provides that a violation of this provision where the victim of the trafficking was under 18 years of age at the time of the commission of the offense is punishable by imprisonment in the state prison for 4, 6, or 8 years. This bill would provide that any person who commits human trafficking involving a commercial sex act where the victim of the human trafficking was under 18 years of age at the time of the*

commission of the offense shall be punished in addition by a fine of not more than $100,000, to be used as specified."[10]

While Chelsea's Law is not in regard only to human trafficking victims, its enactment provides additional punishments and financial retribution requirements from those convicted.

During former Governor Schwarzenegger's time in office, he has led the way on a number of human trafficking measures at the state level. Bill AB 17, signed in 2009, is of particular importance. As a press release from the governor's office stated, specifically, "AB 17 increases financial penalties on those convicted of human trafficking by 400 percent bringing the fine to $20,000 and allows law enforcement to seize assets connected to traffickers, which can greatly increase the financial loss for traffickers. Half of what is collected in fines and seizures will also be made available to community-based organizations that serve underage victims of human trafficking."[11]

Additional noteworthy accomplishments from former Governor Schwarzenegger's time in office include:

- *Bill AB 22, which made human trafficking a felony in California punishable by up to eight years in state prison.*

- *enacting legislation to grant further rights to victims of human trafficking and establishing a pilot program to provide standardized training curricula on the sexual exploitation of minors.*

- *Bill AB 1278, which prohibits contracts that funnel future earnings to pay for the costs of transporting an individual to the US.*

- *signing a joint statement in 2006 with then-Mexican President Vicente Fox, promising cooperation on border security solutions including combating human trafficking along the US-Mexico border.*

- Bill SB 1569, which extends support services like Medi-Cal and Healthy Families to victims of human trafficking.[12]

POSITIVE COMMUNITY EFFORTS

In addition to policy changes are the numerous organizations and coalitions that fight various aspects of human trafficking in California. Perhaps the longest-running coalition effort has been the Bilateral Safety Corridor Coalition (BSCC). In 1993, Marisa Ugarte was working at a program for runaway teenagers when she came across a girl who had been prostituted. Marisa realized that the girl, like many of the women and children who sell their bodies on the streets, was not doing so voluntarily. Rather, this girl and others like her were being commercially exploited by traffickers and pimps. Unlike drugs that were only good for one hit, sex could be sold and resold repeatedly to maximize the profit margin.

Over time, Marisa investigated the underworld of trafficking and connected with grassroots organizations working against trafficking in both San Diego and Tijuana, Mexico. She learned that individuals were being transported against their will, with California as one of many destinations.

Marisa came across rape camps in San Diego, forced labor in agricultural fields, and children exploited in Tijuana's infamous Zona Norte. She began to envision a "safety corridor." Through a UNICEF conference on human trafficking, Marisa was introduced to coalition building and the advantages of strategically pulling resources to create a continuum of services for victims. The BSCC officially launched in 1997 and now includes more than 150 national and international partnerships working in the region that fights human trafficking at its roots.[13]

One of the many outstanding partners fighting human trafficking in Southern California is the Orange County Human Trafficking Task Force (OCHTTF). The tastk force was founded in 2004 and is a collaboration of law enforcement, nongovernmental organizations, faith-based organizations, and the community. Its purpose is, "to work together to protect victims, prosecute offenders, and prevent further perpetration of this crime in Orange County." Represented with a wide variety of partners, lead agencies include Westminster Police Department, CSP Inc. Victim Assistance Programs, Assistant United States Attorney, Federal Bureau of Investigation (FBI), Immigration and Customs Enforcement (ICE), the Salvation Army, and Public Law Center.[14]

What I appreciate most about the work of this particular task force is its focus not only on awareness, but also victim services. The OCHTTF has served more than 60 potential victims of trafficking from 2006 to 2009. This is more than any single county task force we have found in our research to date covering the same period of time. (There may be larger numbers by task forces in New York City, but this is the largest of any one-county network we have seen.) One particular victim served was a young girl named Shyima, who became Orange County's first federal prosecution of a human-trafficking case, culminating in October 2006.

According to the account by Greg Hardesty in *The Orange County Register*, the case began when a 12-year-old girl was found "shabbily dressed with reddish hands caked with dead, hard-looking skin — the result of being forced to work as a domestic servant for a large Irvine family."

The couple lived in a gated community and treated Shyima as an outcast, forcing her to care for their five children and do housework for no pay. According to Shyima, "What they did to me will scar me for the rest of my life. . . . They treated me like nothing."[15]

The sentencing included ordering the couple to pay the girl more than $152,000 in restitution which totaled the amount, plus penalties, that prosecutors calculated she would have made working seven days a week for 20 months. The husband was sentenced to three years in federal prison. His former wife, who also apologized to the court for her treatment of the girl, was sentenced to 22 months. Both were scheduled for deportation to Egypt after serving their sentences. According to the account, Shyima, who comes from an impoverished family, began working in the couple's home in Egypt when she was only nine years old.[16]

Her foster parents adopted Shyima shortly following the verdict. She is now a student, pursuing her dreams with a new life of freedom.

LABOR SLAVES

This particular account also provides an opportunity to discuss the *variety* of trafficking cases, both in California and beyond. Christine Buckley, coauthor with Aaron Cohen of the groundbreaking anti-trafficking book *Slave Hunter*, spoke with an Orange County publication regarding her research on trafficking as it relates to the local area:

> I'm sure there are still slaves working in the local massage (a.k.a. prostitution) parlors and nail salons, but also in restaurants and private homes as domestics. Slaves are everywhere (remember, as many as 17,000 new slaves are brought into this country every year, which means there are somewhere around 50,000 slaves in the U.S. at any one time), and anywhere from 40 percent to 50 percent of them are NOT sex slaves (the media tends to focus on this because it gets big ratings/hits).
>
> Let's not forget about the agricultural workers brought in under false pretenses and held by force or threats in the fields of California, Florida, Texas, and elsewhere while they pick our tomatoes and oranges. Most people do not want to know why certain items they buy are so cheap. The answer is that somewhere along the line, someone is not getting paid. We now have the resources to investigate slave labor in corporations' supply chains. Some corps [corporations] have agreed to do so, but many others have not yet signed on. The good news is that no major industry has more than 2 percent to 3 percent slave labor in its supply chain. So boycotting is not the answer; this will just harm all of the farmers. The solution is to call upon the corporations to take responsibility for what's happening even on the bottom rung of their supply chain . . .
>
> I really think it's important to stress that there are many kinds of slaves, not just sex slaves. And also crucial for you to give readers the tools they need to identify victims and help prevent the slavery that is prevalent in all of our communities. Once we tune into it, we can't help but see it. Once we've seen it, we're unable to forget it, and so we refuse to tolerate it . . . and next thing

you know, the traffickers and slaveholders will be forced to find themselves a new business. And America will truly be the land of the free.[17]

This "variety" of new slavery in California was also the origin of one of the nation's leading anti-trafficking organizations — the Not for Sale campaign — that fueled some of our early research. Several years ago, David Batstone and his wife regularly dined at an Indian restaurant near their home in the San Francisco area. In his words, "Unbeknownst to us, the staff at Pasand Madras Indian Cuisine who cooked our curries, delivered them to our table, and washed our dishes were slaves."[18]

Once the tragic news broke, David found himself motivated to create change in this area. From his perspective, "This was happening in my country at a restaurant I frequented. My shock turned into a consuming passion that took me around the world to learn more about how slavery flourishes in the shadows." The result was the formation of the Not for Sale organization and book by the same title. His efforts represent what he calls "open source activism," or the use of technology and collaborative efforts to connect and mobilize large numbers of ordinary people to do something extraordinary to stop human trafficking.[19]

CAST-LA, cited earlier in this chapter, has provided its own services to trafficking victims for well over a decade. A comparative "veteran" in the field of antitrafficking aftercare, they have helped those in the most desperate situations return to normal life. One example, from trafficking survivor Lulu (not her real name), illustrates the type of work CAST-LA does:

> *Lulu is in her thirties and was illegally brought to Los Angeles in 2008 from her home country in Asia by a labor trafficking operation under FBI investigation. Lulu was an educated Asian woman who believed she was coming to America for a legitimate job opportunity. When she arrived, she realized that she had been sold into slavery. Through repeated physical and sexual abuse, traffickers broke her. When she was rescued, she was in a corner of the house that was being raided, holding on to a teddy bear.*

> *Lulu obtained a Work Authorization card one month after*
> *coming to CAST, which allowed her to find a steady job with an*
> *employer that treated her well. Lulu saved money and was able to*
> *enroll part-time in a nursing program. "When I was with my*
> *[previous] employer, I did the same thing everyday, I was stuck. I*
> *did not feel hopeful of what my future was going to be because I could*
> *not see what was going to happen tomorrow. Now, I feel hopeful.*
> *I can dream. I can see myself doing something with my life in two*
> *weeks, in two months. I am free now."[20]*

Further, a growing number of local churches in the state of California are working to create change in standing against human trafficking. For example, Not for Sale's 2009 Global Forum was held in a California church, complete with music by popular Christian artists. Saddleback Church, one of the nation's largest churches, led by mega-bestselling author Rick Warren, held its first conference featuring human trafficking in 2010 (at Radicalis). On the ground level, members of the Victory Outreach Church of Oakland go to the streets weekly to try to reach women and girls working as prostitutes. On any given night they meet more than a dozen teens and young women working as prostitutes, according to church members. "We're just letting them know there's a destiny for their life," said Sylvia Vigil, wife of the church's pastor. "Basically they're all victims."[21]

On a larger scale, Air1, a Christian radio network based in California with stations nationwide, became a sponsor of Not for Sale's Freedom Tour concert series in an effort to create awareness about modern-slavery and human trafficking.

But perhaps the most direct effort to assist survivors of human trafficking in California is an aftercare center in the San Diego area called Generate Hope. Responding to the report that San Diego has been identified by the FBI as a high intensity child prostitution area and is an international gateway for sex trafficking, Generate Hope opened to serve at least some of those otherwise uncared for through current systems.

"We're very excited to be opening this long-awaited program, as housing for these victims in San Diego is insufficient and until now, there has been no specific treatment available for them," said Executive

Director Susan Munsey. "We'll be filling a very important need for a population that has largely fallen through the cracks." Through featured sponsorships with Harbor Presbyterian Church, North Coast Church, and the SA (Servants Anonymous) Foundation, along with many other partners, young women rescued from sex trafficking in the San Diego area now have at least one place developed by Christians where healing can take place.[22]

GAINING GROUND

At the start of our research on California, we faced an onslaught of reports documenting agricultural slavery, domestic servants in bondage, sweatshops, and various sex trafficking cases that at first led us to believe the state was indeed a hotbed of trafficking activity in an environment where few were doing much to stop it. However, on further investigation, we have found an interesting and growing tension between the criminal element supporting human trafficking in California and an emerging movement of citizens standing against it. More than in any state in our research, individuals, churches, and other organizations are working to defend the cause of the modern slave through public policy changes, prevention, education, awareness, aftercare, and a host of other responses.

Of course, California is also an enormous state geographically, economically, and in population. Some parts of the state, especially the San Diego region, have responded due to local incidents that can no longer be denied or downplayed. San Francisco, always involved in progressive change issues, has become an early adopter in many aspects of the anti-trafficking movements. Orange County and other Southern California communities have stepped up in a variety of ways to create tougher leadership in fighting human trafficking. This combination of government, nonprofits, and everyday citizens each doing something to create change could stand as an example for other states and communities working to eliminate trafficking in their communities. However, at this stage, human trafficking remains prevalent and will continue to challenge the state and its people to go much further in dismantling the apparatus supporting California's modern slave trade.

California has done well to be among one of the first states to rise to the challenge of modern slavery and human trafficking. We hope to see it become one of the first states to experience dramatic change in the number of trafficking victims rescued and prevented in the days ahead.

CHAPTER 7:

EVERYTHING IS BIGGER IN TEXAS, INCLUDING SLAVERY

C☆H☆A☆R☆L☆E☆S

TEXAS IS A HUB

- The National Human Trafficking Hotline, Texas is second only to California in number of calls received each year.[1]
- The Department of Justice designated the I-10 corridor as the *number one route* for human trafficking in the US.[2]

WHENEVER I DESCRIBE the heat in Houston I usually do so using a line from Neil Simon's play *Biloxi Blues*.

"It was hot—Africa hot."

And when I use that line I am not even speaking of the days, but rather referring to the nights, since most of the time I was a police officer in Houston I worked the midnight shift.

THE MIDNIGHT SHIFT

On 8-8-88, I was sworn in as a Texas police officer for one of the many police agencies in Houston. I always thought that was a very interesting date to become employed, as if that day held some special kind of synchronicity. The agency I worked for was just one of more than 78 separate law enforcement agencies in Harris County, which includes Houston, currently the fourth largest city in the United States.

During my time in Houston I encountered almost every crime covered in the Texas Penal Code, including murder, rape, robbery, shootings, prostitution, gang crimes, tons of drugs, and burglary. For most of my years there, I worked the night shift where only one thing was constant. Around 1:00 A.M. every night, while the good citizens of Houston slept peacefully in their beds, only two groups of people remained on the streets: police officers and dangerous criminals who live in the shadows of our suburban nightmares.

Back in the late 1980s and early 1990s the city was different than it is today. The police department had done a great job of shutting down almost all of the overt prostitution all across the city. "Johns" were afraid to approach a suspected prostitute for fear she might be an undercover police officer.

The great social ill and enemy when I worked the streets was crack cocaine. The violence and mayhem was so bad at that time, the local FOX television station started a nightly news program called "City Under Siege" to highlight the death toll and other effects of the gang wars. The problem was so severe that the television program ran for years. The gangs were brazen and fearlessly flew their colors, fighting pitched street battles with one another for control of the drug trades, then fighting the police for control of the streets. As for the police, we were our own kind of gang and fought proudly in the name of law and order and for the sake of innocent citizens. Sadly, the law enforcement community lost several good officers during this period who are now all but forgotten.

I worked as a police officer in Houston for six years. My law enforcement career ended one night in 1993 when a drunk driver ran a stop sign and T-boned my brand-new patrol car at an intersection in Houston's infamous Fourth Ward. I was taken by ambulance to Ben Taub Hospital with a closed head injury, damage to my ankle, neck, and back. It took many years of healing for me to recover physically as well as emotionally from the events of that night.

MEETING THE PALMERS

After 13 years, I recently returned to Houston to investigate human trafficking in the northwest Houston community known as Spring. The day that Mark and Sandra Bass Palmer of Home of Hope-Texas picked me at George Bush Intercontinental Airport, Houston was home to more than 130 brothels, "spas," and strip clubs, many of which were suspected to be trafficking foreign nationals and American citizens for the purposes of some form of sex trafficking or sexual slavery. The Palmers invited me to investigate the problem of human trafficking in Houston where their Home of Hope-Texas nonprofit works daily to build an aftercare facility to rescue and restore victims of sex trafficking and slavery.

To meet Sandra Palmer is to meet a human dynamo, a one-woman wrecking crew, compassion, mercy, and persuasion in high heels. I hadn't even settled into their van before her husband, Mark, sped off from the airport, driving with purpose. Not even a, "Hello, how was your flight?"

Sandra turned around in her seat and started preaching the problems of human trafficking across the Greater Houston area, complete with a map of Houston-area brothels in one hand and a Home of Hope-Texas newsletter in the other. She told me stories from regional law enforcement of women and young girls from abroad as well as in the United States being forced to work as sexual slaves throughout the city. Innocent individuals were being treated by the justice system like criminals instead of victims when the brothels were raided. Sandra also told me about federal funds which were being denied to any rescue efforts, like Home of Hope, that identified themselves in any way as Christian. The funds, earmarked by Congress to be used by rescue facilities, were instead being used to mount a city-wide billboard campaign. Yes, the money was wasted on billboards instead of beds in a rehabilitation facility like Home of Hope, all while adult and juvenile victims alike languished in jail.

She also shared her dream of rescuing underage victims of human trafficking from Channelview to Katy and from Kingwood to Missouri City. She affectionately referred to them as "her girls." In her mind, she was already on the way to provide their rescue. Within minutes Mark Palmer had navigated us from the airport to an area of Highway FM 1960 running through Spring. There was my first glimpse of Houston's most incessant vice pandemic. In strip centers, mini-malls, and free-standing buildings, I saw spas and massage parlors gleaming like beacons of shame, extending mile after mile.

Within an hour the Palmers rented a car for my use during my investigation and took me to a private location (which I cannot reveal) from which to carry out my work against brothels in Houston. Having previously determined to investigate areas along I-45 North and the FM 1960 Highway corridor, there was no need to begin work right away, allowing me to enjoy the evening and share a delicious Tex-Mex dinner with the couple. Mark told me Sandra always feeds people when she meets them and then said, "Once she feeds you . . . you belong to her!" I simply enjoyed the meal and the conversation with this invigorating couple working on the front edge of ending trafficking in their local community.

The following morning the sun burned intensely and by midday the temperature rose to the low 60s, which would have felt great in San Francisco, but the ever-present coastal humidity cooked me from the inside out. Houston is still Houston, even in the winter. By noon I had already staked out four spas and massage parlors along FM 1960 and I-45. It didn't take me long to form an opinion that sex trafficking was absolutely present in the area and that the potential for human trafficking in northwest Houston was just as thick as the humidity.

THE CHALLENGE OF LOCAL ENFORCEMENT

Houston spa and massage parlor businesses are not unlike other cities I have visited in the past two years, other than the fact that in Houston, the organized criminal element has completely perfected its game. The fourth largest city in the United States is considered a wide open city with regard to prostitution: "wide open" meaning criminal organizations operate without fear of prosecution. Sex traffickers have so inundated the city with their presence that it is all but impossible for local, county, state, and federal law enforcement officials to keep up with trafficking activities.

Earlier in this writing I stated there were 130 brothels operating in Houston. That number only represents the verified statistics, yet many in the anti-trafficking movement believe the actual number might be more than twice as high. The law enforcement community in Houston and across Texas has its back against the wall when it comes to sex trafficking, much in the same way it did when crack cocaine first hit the streets.

In writing these facts I am in no way attempting to demean the local or state police in Texas. Usually I have more cause to blame our federal government and bureaucrats that ignore and under-fund the issue of human trafficking. Even still, there is some research to establish that local law enforcement officials across the US are often not willing or have not been trained to recognize human trafficking in their town.

Northeastern University's Institute on Race and Justice (IRJ) surveyed approximately 3,000 state, county, and municipal law enforcement agencies in the US in an effort to gauge the "current perceptions of local law enforcement agencies about human trafficking and also to measure the regularity in which they investigate such cases."[3] The institute's report presented several significant findings:

- *The majority of local law enforcement officers perceive human trafficking as rare or non-existent in their local communities.*

- *Law enforcement most often learns about cases of human trafficking during the course of other criminal investigations.*

- *Agencies associated with federally-funded human trafficking task forces were more than twice as likely to file federal charges when compared to other non-task force agencies.*

- *Law enforcement agencies participating in federally-funded human trafficking task forces that investigated a case of human trafficking reported investigating many more cases on average than non-task force agencies.*[4]

Jurisdictions that come across human trafficking victims may not have adequate means to carry out investigations and prosecutions, nor to provide sufficient social services, particularly in rural communities.

The research indicates that human trafficking cases are multifaceted and resource-driven. If faced with a large group of victims, smaller jurisdictions may be too overwhelmed to prosecute human trafficking violations. In a May 2008 prostitution raid of two Beaumont, Texas, spas, local investigators uncovered a possible human trafficking operation.[5] The Beaumont detectives were working with the FBI, which has jurisdiction in international human trafficking cases, but noted they "don't have the kind of resources to dedicate to this kind of offense."[6] Budgets are already stretched and priorities may be placed on other criminal priorities, such as drug enforcement and homeland security.

Human trafficking victims are regularly discovered by local law enforcement authorities who are investigating other criminal activity, but these agencies do not always recognize potential human trafficking cases. In many situations this might be due to prevailing attitudes as indicated by the IRJ research noted above. Yet in other instances, when training has been provided to local law enforcement, human trafficking is identified and appropriate measures are taken to begin the investigation and to secure a variety of necessary services for the victim. Human trafficking also may be uncovered as a result of joint efforts with federal agencies in the area, such as Immigration and Customs Enforcement (ICE) or the FBI. Providing victim services becomes difficult when the collaborative systems are not in place to handle a human trafficking case. In some cases, service providers and non-governmental organizations, such as a faith-based organization or a domestic violence shelter, may be the first to come in contact with potential human trafficking victim.

Law enforcement agencies also face unique challenges properly identifying foreign-born individuals once they are identified as victims of human trafficking. Trafficking victims are often classified as offenders, and they are usually reluctant to report human trafficking for many reasons, including their fear of law enforcement and potential deportation. Victims fear their traffickers and sometimes do not realize they are victims of crime. Without proper training on the detection of human trafficking and without sufficient resources for investigations, human trafficking may go undetected. Victims will simply be arrested and merely prosecuted as prostitutes. Many foreign victims have been deported, never having received critical services that are needed for recovery.

UNDERCOVER IN SPRING

After staking out spas and massage parlors throughout the morning, by the afternoon I had selected a number of locations to enter, acting as a potential customer using standard methods. On FM 1960 I found a particular shopping center that housed two different spas. I entered the parking lot as far away from the spas as possible and found a safe vantage point where I watched the area for a time. My vigilance soon paid off. I observed a man in his early 40s sitting in a Ford F-150 pickup truck parked in an area of the lot which afforded him the ability to see the entrances to both brothels. It appeared to me that he was dividing his time and attention between them.

I knew right away by the look of him that this man was either a cop or a criminal; I didn't yet know which. There was only one way to find out more. I decide to enter each of the spas, investigate them, then carefully observe him as he observed me. I am usually never in any of the massage parlors or spas more than five minutes before I am ejected for not being willing to choose a woman and pay for services.

I entered the first spa, the one nearest the pickup, and inside found that the business looked very much like a traditional Asian spa, including a Buddhist shrine with food offerings and incense at the entrance near an ATM machine. The one difference was the three women working at the time were all American Caucasians. I had never experienced that before, but it did appear that the women were, at least to some degree, living at the establishment. Two of the women were sleeping as if they had worked the previous night. I was greeted by the third woman who appeared very tired.

The conversation as best I can recall is recorded as follows:

CP: Hi there, my name is Chuck. What's your name?

HER: Wendy. The door fee for a half hour is $30 and the whole hour is $60.

CP: Are these the only girls working today?

HER: (Yawning) Do you see any others?

CP: Well . . . no, I don't.

HER: What's it gonna be? Thirty dollars or $60 or the door?

It was the door.

It's always the door, but this time I had learned something extremely valuable. The place was likely owned by an Asian crime group who had for some reason started using women from the US, women who either knew right now that they were already imperiled or would soon know that to be the truth. I was certain that the women were not trafficked from another country, but there were several signs that the women might be working for an organized criminal group. The "no name brand" ATM in the lobby was one strong indicator. Many men use such privately owned ATMs only to have their bank accounts drained later. Many of these men never report the theft to the police because of the place in which the crime took place.

Interestingly, my quick departure from the ABC Spa got me a very quizzical look from the man in the truck. Apparently most men stayed with Wendy longer than two minutes. I made my way to my truck and drove the short distance to the ZZZ Spa on the other side of the parking lot. The ZZZ Spa was also a very traditional Asian spa. I was greeted at the door by a friendly woman who took me to a room all the way in the back of the building, then told me, "Woman come in soon."

The room was very dimly lit and it took about 30 seconds for my vision to adjust.

Within two minutes I was joined by a very tired looking Asian woman who appeared older than her actual years. Here stood a woman of about 30 who seemed to lack any emotion. She approached me without the usual forced smile, nodded, and gestured toward the bed in the corner of the room and said, "Me Kim."

I could not move.

Something was wrong. This was not like the other places I had visited. Everything *looked* the same and was working the same, but something wasn't quite right. I have investigated dozens of massage parlors and spas across the United States, but it seemed that something even more sinister than usual was going on in this place.

Again she nodded and gestured toward the bed. This time she spoke in low tone, "Me Kim . . . $200 we sex . . . long time you like."

I snapped out of my frozen state and refocused on the situation. "Hi, my name is Chuck. What's your name?"

She said nothing in response to my question, but appeared to be searching for some other words she just didn't have. She spoke no English; likely another recently trafficked woman.

I began my cover story. "I'm from Alabama. Where are you from?"

She shook her head as if to indicate frustration, but not anger, and spoke again, two hundred dollars please . . . for sex."

She looked desperate for a moment and then hurried out of the room. I didn't know if she was going out to get some security guy and whether or not he would have a gun or if I would have to fight my way out of the ZZZ Spa. When she returned she brought the spa's "mamasan" back with her. Unfortunately, the mamasan didn't speak English much better than Kim.

"This is Kim. She take good care of you . . . long love," said the mamasan. She nervously divided her attention between me and some ominous entity outside the door, just down the hallway. She seemed very frightened that at any moment someone or something was going to burst through the door and cause some damage.

I looked closely at her face and through the fear, I saw something else — two black eyes. Then I looked back at Kim and saw bruises on her upper arms in the places I used to look for bruises on battered women when I was street cop. These were the kind of bruises made when someone of superior strength grabs a woman by both arms to shake and control her. The same way a woman is grabbed hard just before she is punched in the face or slapped.

"You give money for girl . . . Kim good girl . . . Kim love man very good . . . you pay now." Again, her words were not a sales pitch because I have heard that many times. The mamasan was pleading with me not to walk. She was desperate to make a sale out of real fear and still I hadn't answered her. That's what I do. I stall and I try to observe as much as I can for as long as I can, but this time it was different. I would not and could not offer them money even if I paid and walked. I will not underwrite organized crime.

She tried one last time. "You pay now $200 and you get love by Kim and mamasan . . . two women . . . you pay now."

Outside in the hallway there was the sound of a door opening and someone walking down the hall. This made both the mamasan and Kim bristle with fear and then it all came together for me. These women were being used by some criminal organization that required a daily or weekly minimum payment and obviously this location had fallen behind. The rough treatment and black eyes were courtesy of whoever was in the hallway. They were bargaining with me for cash in an effort to prevent further beatings.

It was time to go.

I *had* to leave. Besides, I wanted to see who was in the hallway, creating such fear in these two women. I passed by Kim and the mamasan, pushed open the door, and made my way into a hallway. The perennial smells of an Asian brothel hit my nose like a fist. Incense. Overcooked rice. Pine-scented disinfectant.

The hallway was even darker than the room I'd been in and again my eyes slowly adjusted. Through the darkness I peered toward the front of the building's sunlit entrance where I saw a person standing near the entrance — a person who was now standing in the middle of the hallway, blocking my exit. Sunlight framed the human obstruction at the end of the hall. Just beyond whatever or whoever stood there was daylight and freedom, at least for me. Who knew what was going to happen to the two poor souls I was forced to leave in the room behind me?

As my eyes adjusted to the light and the shape before me took on a more well-defined human form, I found myself no more than two feet from the object of absolute terror for mamasan and Kim.

She was about 50 years old.

She stood about 5 feet, 5 inches tall and wore a very traditional Asian dress. Her arms were folded across her chest in some form of mock defiance. Mainly because I had not bent to her will by spending money to participate in the organized rape she profited from 24 hours a day.

I wanted to rage against this woman for the humanitarian disaster she was perpetrating, but I was not to be her judge that day. Rather, I had just become a witness.

I walked past the "Dragon Lady," outside into the sunlight.

I was safe.

I was free.

But I was shaken on the inside.

My mandate was to investigate human trafficking and pimp-forced prostitution in the United States and to do so for a year in order to develop a model for rescuing victims. Even still, how can I leave someone behind I believe is a slave? Kim and the mamasan would likely face repercussions, but leaving them behind hurt me deeply as well.

I will never know what happened to them.

I think of them often.

I have added them to the host of other human memories that visit me almost every night just after I drift to sleep; those unforgiving thoughts that remind me I was unable to save victims from many circumstances not of my own creation.

Rape victims. Abused child. Gunshot fatalities. Those who had overdosed on drugs.

From time to time while I sleep they all stand in line and wait their turn to ask me why I didn't rescue them before it was too late. Doctors call my struggle one of the many effects of PTSD (post-traumatic stress disorder). It is common among soldiers, cops, firemen, and other first responders who gaze too long into the worst that humanity can do to others. But I can no longer share a peaceful night of sleep while women like Kim are held in animal-like conditions.

As I drove away from the ZZZ Spa, I drove right past the man who was still watching. I slowed my vehicle to a crawl when I came even with the pickup so I could look into his eyes. This simple yet powerful act took him back a bit and appeared to make him very uncomfortable. If he was a criminal I was angry at him for playing some part in all of the wrong taking place in that shopping center. If he was a cop I was angry that while he was outside on a stakeout, women were being beaten, abused, and worse in brothels within his sight and he was either unwilling or unable to do anything about it.

Later that evening I met Mark and Sandra Palmer for a meeting at a local church. When I was called upon to make my presentation I pulled out my laptop computer and got the usual looks from those who expected the cerebral PowerPoint presentation. But their looks changed to shock when I showed them visual evidence pointing to human trafficking within three miles of where they were seated.

Sandra and Mark were thankful for the evidence and perhaps more grateful to have an audience that was now completely riveted.

The response from others in attendance ran the gamut from, "I can't believe that spa is so near the church. Something must be done!" to, "Hey, buddy, why'd you have to go and tell what I didn't really want to know?" I also passed around copies of several free newspapers that can be found in their community's adult bookstores, strip clubs, and some restaurants. The cover of one of these publications featured an ad for a spa just off of I-45 North. The most prominent feature of the ad was a picture of a girl who could not have been older than 13 or 14 years old. I guess that in Houston, things have degraded to the point that these brothels actually place pictures of children in their advertisements. What's worse, newspapers feel the freedom to print the ads that come very close to child pornography. Thank God for people like Sandra Palmer who stood up from among the crowd to stand against this great evil.

THE LOSS OF A FRIEND

A few months ago, I was cooking dinner when my cell phone rang. On the other end of the phone was Dillon.

"Charles, have you heard from Mark Palmer?"

"No," I said, "Should I have heard from him?"

Dillon proceeded to tell me that just before 6:00 P.M. on Friday, April 23, 2010, Sandra was in Lower Swatara Township, Pennsylvania, for a speaking engagement when the minivan she was traveling in was struck from behind by an 18-wheeler. The van was crushed into a tree and both Sandra and the woman driving were killed instantly.[7]

Mark's wife was gone.

My new friend Sandra, dead.

The driving force and public face behind Home of Hope-Texas passed away one week after negotiating space in a building with another nonprofit. This new facility, when opened, will create bed space for 25 victims of sex trafficking and domestic minor sex trafficking. It was almost as if her victory had come with a personal price tag. My fondest memory of Sandra will always be walking with her around the Home of Hope property as she shared her vision of the buildings they would construct and the many children they would help. As we walked she said things like, "This is where my girls will run and play and learn the dignity of freedom." Sandra would have laid her life down to save a child. That is certain.

Instead, she died while traveling to tell people about the need to create a place like the Home of Hope-Texas. I am saddened that the money allocated by the federal government for helping victims in Houston is being spent on billboards and media campaigns instead of individual girls like Kim. Sandra and Mark recounted to me several stories of those who refused to give their organization the money which was specifically earmarked for new facilities to be built because of the Christian purposes which are a part of their rescue plans. This forced Sandra to undertake a grueling public speaking and fundraising schedule across the United States to obtain the necessary funds to build the Home of Hope-Texas. Her sacrifice and dedication eventually cost Sandra her life.

One day, when the foundations are poured and the cornerstone is laid to start construction of the new facility, Sandra's dream will become reality.

When I visited the Home of Hope property I looked for the deer that roam freely there. They have been so crowded by suburban sprawl that the only sanctuary they have left is the heavily wooded Home of Hope-Texas property. I remember marveling that although the deer were completely wild they were very comfortable with Sandra and always lingered whenever she was near. I like to stroll where I once walked with Sandra. Each time the breezes blow through the trees I pause and spy the deer as they turn their heads and I can almost hear God's voice whispering hope and help and peace . . . for Sandra's girls and all God's creatures.

Sandra's compassionate spirit changed the lives of many. Her legacy will continue to impact future generations through helping girls like Kim and others experience true and lasting freedom.

CHAPTER 8:

INTERSTATE NETWORKED TRAFFICKING

C☆H☆A☆R☆L☆E☆S & D☆I☆L☆L☆O☆N

CHONG KIM IS a bright young woman in her 30s. She lives in Texas. Chong is a conference speaker, writer, a wife, and mother. Plus, she loves her cats. But there's one unique aspect of Chong's life that many do not know.

Chong Kim is also a survivor of human trafficking.

I had the opportunity to speak with Chong one fall afternoon. Her experiences as a trafficking victim represent everything about the crime that many people just don't understand. It often requires a significant criminal organization to successfully traffic women across the United States. Once a person has been sucked into the system, it can be difficult and sometimes deadly to escape. Chong's story explains how an evil so dark can take place in our own communities as well as the hope that exists for those who survive. Further, her story is one of many examples in which not only one community, but multiple communities are involved in the trafficking of one individual. Though much of our book highlights this problem at the community or city level, one of the more common traits of American sex trafficking is that women are moved to a variety of locations along various circuits, possibly passing through your very own community.

A SURVIVOR'S STORY

Chong Kim's story is powerful in many ways, but one of the most convicting elements is that in her time as a sex slave, she may have passed through my own town without me even knowing.

CP: How did you become a victim of human trafficking?

CK: I was actually kidnapped; I had a gun to my head. The head person that does the trafficking was a consultant with the FBI in Las Vegas. So it was very corrupt.

CP: You were kidnapped? Start there; tell me about it.

CK: It started out, I actually met the guy and I thought he was my boyfriend. I didn't realize he was a recruit. The way the trafficking was set up, it's where they send out these young boys all the way through college-age to look for young girls to dote on them until they get their trust. I didn't realize that I was one of them, one of the girls that was picked for this whole trafficking scenario. This guy, I really believed he cared. It was here in Dallas, Texas, that I met him. From there we went to northern Oklahoma. That's where I was handcuffed to a doorknob in an abandoned house and was kept there for approximately three to six months. He was getting angry and he [didn't] follow their directions and so they [the traffickers] sent a backup person. The backup person was a woman.

CP: Tell me about her. What was she like?

CK: This woman was white, she was probably in her early 40s, and probably was a madam herself. So she was the one who basically came to pick me up, and I thought she was rescuing me from a domestic violence situation. That's what I thought it was. And I trusted her. She said she was going to help me run away and she in turn, was the person that sent me to the trafficker. And she got paid for it.

CP: So after northern Oklahoma, where were you taken?

CK: To Las Vegas, Nevada.

CP: What happened when you arrived in Las Vegas?

CK: We were taken to an abandoned warehouse district and one of those warehouses; it's not like one of the outdoor warehouses, where each unit is on the outside. This was an abandoned warehouse unit where the units were inside the building.

So anything that went on, nobody would see and it was private property. Before the cops can go in, they have to see probable cause. If there's no probable cause, no one's going to step in and no one's going to know there's anything going on.

CP: There's no case to make.

CK: Exactly, exactly. So, we were in a rural area in the desert. Whenever I was there, each unit held different types of girls. [First] Caucasian girls [from outside the US], and second were American Caucasian girls, and they were being sent to Amsterdam, Sweden, Germany, London, that's where they were being sent to. The other girls [from outside the US], they were being sent to different countries. [Third,] the minority immigrant girls were being brought here to the United States because if you look at, you know very well that with the drug distribution it's all about trade — bringing in and bringing out. What you put in the US and what you put out of the US. That was the same thing with human trafficking.

CP: You're in this place and they said, "OK, there's a man in here; he's going to give you money and you're going to give him sex." Tell me about your first day to work as a prostitute.

CK: My first day to work as a prostitute we were being taken to the warehouse district. First we had to get on the warehouse truck. We were transported in the warehouse truck, me and the other girls, and they would take us to these motels that they owned. They would hire illegal immigrants to work at the front desk to say "No vacancy." That was their job. To make sure tourists didn't stop by to lounge. They would basically tell them "No vacancy." Each of the rooms was already prepared for me and the customer. There would be the traffickers that would stand outside the hotel, the motels, and the doorknobs were inside out; which means we would be locked in, instead of us locking them out. The windows were boarded up so no one could look into the windows and I couldn't look out. When I walked in, I remember seeing the bed, there was no TV, and no radio, and there was no phone. They would have a TV but it never worked. You know, it wasn't plugged in, or the cord was cut off. But they would just have it for design. They would have our lingerie, or something that we would wear, on the bed, they would have a makeup case in the bathroom and they would tell us to take ten minutes to shower and put our makeup on and then get ready. I remember crying and I was shaking so bad that I kept pounding on the door. If I didn't comply or I talked back they would inject me with some kind of narcotic that would calm me down. And they would inject me in my arm. I remember feeling nauseous, feeling dizzy, and feeling like I couldn't move my body. And I would just be laying there and then the customer would walk in and see me laying there and they would do their job, and then when they were done, a lot of times they would knock on the door and say, "Time's up!" outside the door so the customer would have to put his clothes on and then walk out. Then he would tell me "Get cleaned up, the next one's coming in." That's how it went.

CP: Which kind of criminal organization was this?

CK: Um, it was an international criminal organization, but the majority of the customers were white Americans. And the customers were anywhere between CEOs, lawyers, police officers, we've even had really high-echelon pastors, different types of men. They were high status; there were even political figures that were there that bought me. It was just very disturbing and very disheartening to see the people that we trust were all involved in this.

CP: So what other places were you eventually taken to work?

CK: It was anywhere between Nevada, Los Angeles, New York, Miami, Philly, Florida, and Houston, Texas. They would take us everywhere and we would be in one location probably for a month because we had to move quickly and that was to avoid cops coming after us.

CP: Can you tell me what one of your worst experiences might've been during that time?

CK: Even though I was 18, I was sold as a 13-year-old Japanese girl. So there were men that actually assumed I was a minor and that to me was very, very hard to grasp because I realized, "Oh my gosh, a pedophile is buying me." And he has the money to buy me, and that is so grotesque. The way they think that they are nice to you is because they let you talk a little bit . . . and it was just very disgusting and very sad.

There were times I wanted to throw up. This one particular customer bought me as a 13-year-old and he talked to me in broken English. If I didn't give him what he wanted, if I kept saying, "No, no, me not want," you know, because I had to speak in broken English, he said, "I bought you," and "I deserve," and "I spent my money on you," and "You're nothing." I was called every racist word you can think of. This one guy when he choked me and I started screaming, he said, "Yeah, I've always wanted to hear what a Chinese pig squealed like!" I just felt like I wasn't human anymore. I felt like I was nothing but a product and here was this person destroying the product and he didn't care.

CP: How you were rescued?

CK: I actually wasn't rescued, per se, I ran away, and I definitely want to share why. Before I explain why I ran away, I had to rank up to be a madam. That was the only way to make the big escape because of being a madam. That was when I was able to see everything and how they orchestrated everything, and how, this was the type of trafficking that didn't just do sex trafficking, they were dealing with drugs and trade, just about anything and anyone whether illegal or not illegal, that's what they would do.

CP: So what year was it that you were taken and that you ran away?

CK: In 1995 I was taken and in 1997 was when I ran away.

BILLBOARD MESSAGES

As I wrote in an earlier chapter, I live in north Georgia just outside Atlanta. My house is also close to the South Carolina state line. From almost the moment you cross into the Palmetto State you pass several billboards featuring advertisements for the many massage parlors and spas located from Anderson to Greenville to Spartanburg, all the way to Charlotte, North Carolina. I call it the Carolina Corridor.

I once read that it takes multiple impressions of an advertisement for a product, using various means of presentation, in order to garner any significant amount of attention and affirmative response from consumers in the United States. Yet the same advertisement used in a developing nation requires fewer impressions upon the intended consumer to affect behaviors in a positive manner for the very same product.

Why? In the United States we are continuously overstimulated, whereas in developing countries, apparently the phrase "New and Improved" has yet to reach the point of being easily ignored. Perhaps that plays a part in explaining why many people across the United States peacefully co-exist with prostitution and human trafficking. It is very possible that each day as you drive to work or the mall you pass right by billboards that promote massage parlors and spas where trafficking or prostitution takes place. Yes, there are many legitimate day spas and massage establishments in your city as well, but everything that is legitimate helps that which is illegitimate blend into the background.

But what about those billboards that are clearly not legit? Why do you suppose Asian spas place ads in the sports section of the newspaper? Have you ever read some of the classified ads in the back section of the free local entertainment magazines and papers? If you did, you might find prostitution and even human trafficking among the pages of print, just as it is in upstate South Carolina. In a world of commercialism, it almost becomes an act of emotional survival to pick and choose very carefully which stimuli we allow into our consciousness. It is also just as easy to refuse stimuli that we find morally repugnant. The trouble is that just because we ignore much of the environment around us doesn't mean we cease to live in that ever-increasingly dangerous and base world we no longer notice. That's quite possibly the reason so many people don't know that illegal prostitution and human trafficking are going on in their city, county, or state.

That's all it takes for you to help propagate a national tragedy — what some call the sin of omission. The responses given by thousands of German people when asked about the concentration camps near their cities in fallen Nazi Germany were all the same, "We can't be blamed for this tragedy. . . . We didn't know what all the barbed wire and smoke was about."

This same lack of response is exactly what traffickers are counting on. If I am forced to tell the ugly truth about the numerous massage parlors and spas and their billboard advertisements littering I-85 from the Georgia state line north through South Carolina all the way to Charlotte, North Carolina, I would be remiss if I left out the horrible blight on the landscape in my own beloved Peach State that includes a much more notorious corridor than any found in either of the Carolinas.

If you drive between Macon and Valdosta, Georgia, you will experience 154 miles of Interstate 75 through a mostly rural region of the state. If you drive the speed limit, it will take you a little under three hours to make the trip, just about the amount of time needed to listen to some great Southern blues music (I personally suggest the Muddy Waters Blues Anthology).

As you make your way from one community to the next, I also suggest you have your passenger read every single billboard you pass. If you do so, you will be surprised at the results. At any given time there are more than 70 billboards dedicated solely to promoting sexually oriented businesses such as spas, massage parlors, strip clubs, and adult video stores, all of which are equally offensive whether you are traveling north or south. Often when people view things they find offensive they are initially shocked but become increasingly desensitized upon numerous additional viewings. You might think this would be the case in viewing these billboards, but not so according to a very informal and unscientific test I have performed numerous times over the past two years.

Whenever I have drive this stretch of road with a passenger, I always ask them to read every billboard and count the ones advertising "adult" services or products. Upon the sighting of the first massage parlor sign my passengers usually respond with something like; "Wow, there's one already!" Then by the time we have sighted adult billboard number 10 they are completely shocked at the sheer number of signs in such a short distance. By the time we have driven the entire 154 miles they are usually a mess over the sheer spectacle of mass depravity they had never observed when making the journey on previous occasions.

One of my riders thought there should be a federal investigation on the matter while another person suggested law enforcement was either falling down on the job or in on the criminal activity. A third individual put the blame squarely on the church for allowing adult businesses that profit from prostitution or human trafficking to prosper unchallenged by Christians so deep within the so-called Bible Belt. Regardless of the truth behind these undisputed billboards, the bottom line is that they are still there, day after day, month after month, and year after year with little or no challenge from nearby communities.

In addition, billboards are expensive. These are not situations in which a local pimp decided to increase advertising. An established business with a history, financial surplus, and media connections is generally required to accomplish such a task. Who is taking a stand to stop these activities?

Over the past year, Mercy Movement has begun to speak out on these billboards in Georgia, specifically those in the Macon area where many are concentrated. Other grassroots groups have also begun to take action with fruitful results. If we had written this book a year earlier, we could have provided ample photographs to include Lamar Advertising, which owns two-thirds of the billboards in middle Georgia. Since that time, they have now shown responsibility to stand against companies using their signs to promote the adult services industry. However, as reported in March 2010, Lamar is choosing to allow such billboard contracts to expire quietly, slowly lowering the number of such signs littering middle Georgia highways.

To this, we can gladly say thank you and support this ongoing effort. May others follow this example. However, there are two areas in which we still see grave concern. First, this has been a "phase out" rather than a complete halt. Though perhaps less difficult from a business perspective, the ethics here are difficult to justify. For example, if I knew a sign I leased to a company was supporting prostitution, human trafficking, or even had the potential to do so, I would remove it immediately no matter the financial expense to me personally. Why? In some situations, it could spare a woman from being purchased for sex that day. Anything less shows, to some degree, a lack of seriousness regarding the protection of women in our culture.

Second, it is disheartening and disturbing that the sign company itself would be the source that decided to stop working with companies offering adult services. There are numerous ways state laws, local business groups, individuals, churches, and other organizations could have addressed the issues to push for change rather than waiting for the company to do so. In honesty, some people among these groups did press for change and have helped alter the situation, including our organization, but these numbers are few in the current battle.

In your community, if you see a billboard advertising a business that could be involved in trafficking or illegal prostitution, we challenge you to do something to end it today. First, make sure your facts are accurate (please contact our organization if you need help with research). Second, expose the group. Contact the business leasing the sign and share why they should remove the sign immediately. If they refuse, report the information publicly. Evil enjoys the darkness, but once the company behind the advertising is mentioned in your local paper, on the radio, or on television, action seems to take place more quickly. If needed, rally a group of local people to contact the company and spread the message supporting the need to end advertising to the particular business. In almost all cases, there is a certain tipping point of community involvement that "forces the hand" of the leasing company to end advertising. The changes in middle Georgia are one example where this is taking place on a small scale that can be replicated nationwide.

PROSTITUTION ON PARKWAY EAST

Several months ago I (Charles) took a trip to Birmingham, Alabama, where I spoke to a group of local leaders about the work of Mercy Movement and the topic of human trafficking, illicit spas, massage parlors, and prostitution in general across the US. I prepared for the meeting in the manner that I often prepare. I traveled to Birmingham a day early and studied the city regarding its local connections with human trafficking and any possible connections with forced prostitution and organized crime. It is often valuable to begin my investigation in an area where I can find a concentration of spas and massage parlors. In Birmingham I quickly learned that such an area existed on Parkway East.

I drove around the neighborhood for a time and noted that a number of these spas and massage parlors were located in close proximity to one another. I eventually entered the XXX Spa (not its real name) and used my normal procedures to converse with as many women as possible while observing the location until being asked to either select a woman and pay or leave the establishment. I entered the door to the sound of jingling chimes where I was greeted at the door by a cordial mamasan.

The mamasan began, "Hello. How are you?" She then laughed, trying to show she was good-natured and friendly.

"Hello!" I said.

"Come this way, please," she said, leading me down a darkened hall.

She pointed me to an even darker room and asked, "Have you been here before?"

I answered, "I have never been to any spa before."

"Oh. Sixty dollars please."

I hesitated slightly, expressing a look of confusion (part of my exit strategy). She responded unconcerned.

She repeated her fee, "Sixty dollars."

I responded as if surprised, "Sixty dollars? I don't have $60 with me. My friend told me that it would only be $40. Um, OK?"

She said, "You need ATM?"

"Yes," I said, "Is there one near here?"

"Yes, there is one near here," she said quickly giving me well-rehearsed directions to the nearest ATM machine.

Before I left I tried one last tactic to find out what women were working that evening. "Do you have some pretty girls here?" I asked.

"Yes . . . sure," she said. "You back to room and wait."

I returned to my assigned room. Soon I was met by a woman I am guessing was in her 30s whom I will call Kim.

"Hello, how are you?" she asked.

"Hello, I'm Chuck. What's your name?"

"Kim," I heard through her heavy accent. "You want ATM machine?"

"Yes."

"I'm from Dallas. Where are you from?" I probed.

"I'm from California. LA." She was certainly lying about her hometown just as much as I. She was definitely not from the States and I couldn't resist saying something about it.

"Your accent doesn't sound very much like California," I suggested with a laugh.

She laughed as well.

"Nice to meet you," I said and shook hands with her, hoping to prolong my time and discover more about this woman in a desperate situation. Unfortunately, she was ready to lead me back toward the hallway and out of the room, but she stopped me near the room's doorway and whispered something.

"You bring back $200," she said.

"The other woman said I only needed to pay the $60 door fee," I shrugged curiously.

Then she whispered, "You bring back $200 and you get *everything.*"

For clarity's sake, I feigned bad hearing and asked, "Did you just say that if I bring back $200 you would give me everything?"

Her reply was to smile broadly and simply say, "Everything $200."

Kim then saw me to the door. Chimes jingled again, this time behind me as I walked toward my vehicle and drove back up Parkway East, immediately calling Dillon on my cell phone to share about the incident.

The following day Dillon and I made our presentation and got the usual responses. Some disbelief, some shock, and plenty of "Surely not here!" Some people appreciated what we had to say while there were a few people who thought that some of the presentation was a bit too graphic in its details. I am used to all of these responses so none of it surprised me. But there was one incident of note. After most of the audience had left, a woman who stated she worked with an alliance of anti-trafficking organizations approached Dillon and me. She specifically took some offense to my undercover operation at the XXX Spa. She seemed to think that I might have in some way endangered ongoing law enforcement efforts there.

I told her that nothing I had done could have in any way hurt law enforcement efforts at the XXX Spa or any other spa in Alabama because the answer to the problem is not more law enforcement. There are not enough law enforcement officials on duty, whether federal, state, or local, to stop human trafficking, even if all of them put all of their time 24/7 on the problem. I responded that the answer to ending modern slavery is for individuals, civic groups, and churches to get out in the streets and work through nonviolent public demonstrations.

The young woman was clearly frustrated and proceeded to tell me she was personally aware that in the very near future, XXX Spa was going to be raided and closed once and for all and that following the raid all of the other spas and massage parlors on Parkway East were going to be closed down by law enforcement in association with the groups with which she was aligned. She thought we just didn't "get it." In the end we politely agreed to disagree.

Six months have passed since our conversation with the young woman in Birmingham. Tonight, as I write these words, the only reference I can find to the XXX Spa in Birmingham's leading newspaper, *The Birmingham News*, is a map in the health and beauty section of their Web site announcing the business as a good choice for massage and wellness. I searched multiple databases and found no references to a raid there. However, I did find a brand new ad for the XXX Spa on a Web site catering to men seeking AMPs (Asian massage parlors) where sex is offered for a price. Tonight the ad reads, "Under New Management. Call us for sensual massage. You'll be glad you did." Tonight I also tracked down online ads for other illicit massage parlors and spas that are still operating in the open on Parkway East in Birmingham. Business is not hurting yet for sex traffickers in the area.

My telling of the story is not to demean the efforts of law enforcement and other anti-trafficking groups in Alabama. On the contrary, I fully support local efforts to stand against such activity. But I also know law enforcement alone is not the answer. They will never have enough money or officers to make a dent in the problem. Law enforcement alone is never the answer to a social problem like human trafficking, yet some people still say, "Let the police handle it." Others, like the woman in the above story, take the approach that only their group or coalition knows how to respond.

The Mercy Movement actively seeks to work with and/or know every legitimate individual and organization seeking solutions to the problem of modern-day slavery, especially those working in the US. The most effective advocate is the everyday citizen who gets fed up with a social problem and gets involved. To those like the woman we met in Birmingham I can only say, no one should ever feel so successful and "connected to important people" that they are upset over someone else trying to help. Such humility is required for those of us who desire to see human trafficking removed from our communities. Our success is not found in the right conferences, influential connections, or advanced degrees (as great as those may be), but in the humility that takes an individual from the padded pew to the streets in pursuit of the one person whose life will be changed for eternity through their actions.

I wish it was as easy as simply gathering some evidence and sending in a team to raid a local establishment to end slavery in a community. Some have tried, but the problem is bigger than one location and one crackdown. From demand by "Johns" to ads on billboards to locations to access to women to the money flow involved, it will take involvement on the scale of a civil rights movement from the residents of Birmingham to end trafficking and modern slavery. It happened when Rosa Parks sat in a bus seat in nearby Montgomery, Alabama, to get other people out of their seats to act. It can happen again when people of all backgrounds work together to eliminate modern slavery today.

ONLINE ADVERTISING

Back to billboards. Billboards, of course, are not the only source of advertising in the human trafficking realm. The Internet supports a wide variety of sex crimes. One specific trend we have identified in our own research is closely related to the organized crime and billboard elements mention in this chapter.

Early in our journey, we attempted an analytical composite of the types of ads placed on Craigslist.com (prior to its ending of this category in late 2010) for common themes. What we found that surprised us most was not the graphic nature of the ads, but the locations of the ads. Over a multiweek period in early 2010, we would find that the same exact ads for women listed in Atlanta, Georgia (where we began our study), would be listed the next week in Birmingham, Alabama. The circuit would continue, often clockwise, through Nashville to Charlotte and sometimes dipping down to Orlando before returning to Atlanta.

Other parts of the country expressed their own distinct patterns. We monitored these to a lesser degree, with a noticeable pattern involving Houston to Dallas to Oklahoma City to Memphis, dipping into various Louisiana locations, then back down into Texas. The Pacific Northwest revealed a noticeable focus along the coast between Portland, Oregon, to Vancouver, Canada (Shared Hope International observes a similar and wider network in this region involving domestic minors, including Hawaii, Phoenix, Arizona, Denver, Colorado, and Salt Lake City, Utah). Las Vegas held the highest number of ads among any city during most checks, with heavy traffic between Vegas and California. The Northeast and Midwest did not unearth the same circuits in our observations, though larger cities such as Chicago, New York, and Detroit were destination locations and a much larger than expected population was discernable in Ohio (some speculate a connection between Canada and trafficking with Ohio, but we did not uncover significant evidence either way regarding this suggestion). South Florida had its own unique ads, but did not seem as connected with other circuits internally within the US.

Overall, our focus concentrated on routes orbiting Atlanta that in many ways simply confirmed what FBI reports have publicly shown regarding the city as a major hub for sex trafficking in the region. This included a variety of ethnicities among the ads, with unspecified Asian and American women as the dominant ethnic groups.

Three facts in this research were indisputable. First, major cities are the hubs. Trafficking appears to be almost exclusively a crime flowing from larger cities to smaller ones via interstate highways, not vice versa. Second, airports with high numbers of international routes rank highest with cities featuring the most ads online for foreign women offering sexual services. As such, Atlanta, as the world's busiest airport, would be one of the major spots to investigate, as has been the case in recent years. Orlando; New York; Washington, D.C.; Los Angeles; Miami, Florida; and Houston, Texas, express similar patterns. Though investigators in the past have cited port cities as sources of trafficking, from our observations, airports tend to dominate international sex trafficking in the number of online ads. Third, border states (primarily California, Texas, and Florida) are the states with the highest numbers of reported trafficking victims (sex trafficking and forced labor). As a result, border control and immigration play a larger role than is often noted in sex trafficking.[1]

Again, Craigslist.com is not the only Web site to have promoted such services, but it was the one we investigated that offered the most opportunities for observation. The Washington, D.C.-based Polaris Project has published results from its own studies in 2007 and more recently in 2009 based on the adult services section on Craigslist.com. In short, they consistently found an average of more than 10,000 ads per *day* when counting postings from all cities nationwide.[2] The rate of $10 per ad (lower for repostings) multiplied by these numbers provides a hefty profit while creating a major hub for online sexual services. Certainly not every posting is part of human trafficking, but some are and Craigslist has been making money from it for several years.

In addition, BackPage.com, one of the nation's leading online classified Web sites, features a subscription-based service where users are able to make comments regarding their experiences with particular girls at specific locations. This forum has become so disturbing that recent efforts by anti-trafficking organizations nationwide have helped to push BackPage.com to respond with changes. As of the time this book goes to print, the business has chosen to implement the following changes:

- *The review of all ads and images in the personals and adult sections of the site.*

- *The implementation of key word searches to quickly identify banned advertisements and inappropriate discussions.*

- *The significant increase in staff to quickly identify illegal ads.*

- *The implementation of roadblocks to prevent minors from accessing mature content.*

- *The implementation of dedicated tools on the site to educate users regarding online safety and security.*

- *The empowerment of users to report abuse and an expeditious process to handle user complaints.*[3]

However, anti-trafficking and pro-family groups should continue to monitor this situation as the site only has some portions under review, leaving some areas open where similar ads continue to be posted. Escort and massage listings continue to carry messages that could only refer to prostitution that would include some cases of international or domestic sex trafficking. In fact, in its current state, this "chain" continues as some of the free listings at BackPage.com list ads for subscription-only services outside of their Web site that link to other locations promising the same graphic details. Some even note which exotic massage parlors include ATM machines.

We do not include these details for fun nor do we recommend these Web sites. The point is that American sex trafficking includes a variety of factors that must be ended to reduce and eliminate trafficking in local communities. Certain Web sites, local newspaper ads, interstate billboards, banks offering accounts and ATM machines to adult services locations, leaseholders who provide rental space, and other factors all contribute to a society where such acts take place in a nation that we call the land of the free.

Only together can we work to stand against such evil in our generation.

Further, we must realize the increasing global nature of modern slavery and human trafficking. The US is not immune to trafficking, but is part of a worldwide situation in which millions of people live in bondage today. While the focus of this book has been on trafficking within our nation's borders, along the way we have connected with a variety of partners working to free men, women, and children in difficult situations around the world. In our next chapter, you'll hear some of the stories we are able to share (unfortunately, we cannot share details regarding many others due to safety concerns). We encourage you to be awakened to what is taking place around our world as well as inspired by those who are sacrificing to make a difference through freeing slaves internationally.

CHAPTER 9

BEYOND AMERICA— THE INTERNATIONAL SCENE

C★H★A★R★L★E★S & D★I★L★L★O★N

SUJO JOHN IS famous. Some say he is a hero. He's a well known survivor of September 11, 2001. At 8:45 A.M. on that fateful day he was at work on the 81st floor of the World Trade Center's North Tower. He had just faxed some documents when the building was rocked by a massive explosion from hijacked American Airlines Flight 11, which had crashed into the building. Sujo's thoughts went immediately to his wife who was expecting their first child and worked on the 71st floor of the South Tower. In his words:

> *My heart was sinking. I wondered if the plane had also hit the South Tower where my pregnant wife worked. We fought our way through the fire and made our way to the stairwell. As we were coming down the flights I am trying to reach my wife through my cell phone. But cell phones are not working. . . . As I continued my descent down we now see hundreds of firemen and policemen pass us as they were making their way up. . . . We had no idea then that these brave men were walking up to their death.*[1]

SUJO JOHN'S CALLING

When he finally reached the ground level he walked in the direction of the South Tower in hopes that he might see his wife. Then there was another great explosion followed by the ground shaking all around him as the South Tower collapsed. Large pieces of steel and concrete fell all around him. He and a few other people huddled together and started praying, asking God for strength. Sujo encouraged everyone around him to accept Christ, to call out His name. He and everyone around him were calling upon the name of Jesus. When the building had finished collapsing, Sujo was completely safe without a single injury. Later in the day he discovered that his wife was late for work and never entered the doomed building in which she had been scheduled. When Sujo walked away from the rubble of the Twin Towers he walked away from more than just a disaster. He was changed forever by the experience.

Today Sujo John is still helping people and leading them toward light and safety. Shortly after 9/11, Sujo John accepted the call on his life to become an evangelist and to carry the gospel of Jesus to the world, particularly his home country of India. The second-most populous nation on the planet, India is home to more slaves than any other nation on earth.

In the research for this book, I spoke with Sujo regarding his work. What follows is a portion of his story.

CP: Tell me about your recent trip to India, a quick overview of what you do there. Then tell me about this recent trip dealing with human trafficking.

SJ: Well, you know, I grew up in India, so I go back a lot to preach the gospel and when involved in church planting we work in slums of India, build schools in villages, and we view that as a way to earn the right to preach the gospel. This trip was interesting because for almost six months there's been a couple in New Delhi, the capital of India, and they've been asking me to meet a man who goes into these brothels.

This time I left from the US and we went into this place that is the largest brothel in New Delhi, one of the largest in the world. I think like 3,000 prostitutes live in that area. And I'd never been in a brothel. I'd only seen prostitutes on the streets. But what was interesting in New Delhi, is because prostitution is illegal; they cannot be on the streets. And so we had no idea what else to expect. The moment we stepped on the street, with all the cars, we could just feel their darkness, and it was so dark. And then we were let into this building and the staircases were so dingy. I used a light on my cell phone so that we would not trip. When we get in there, we found these girls, because they couldn't stay on the streets, but were sitting in the stairwell. We went up there and it was a sight I had never experienced. Hundreds of prostitutes, the pimps, the customers, all around; it's a big hallway all sitting together.

CP: Did you see any Westerners there? Or anyone that looked like they were Westerners?

SJ: No, there were no Westerners. Although you talk about Westerners, I think what happens, it's been cut down a lot, at least where India's concerned. I know in Asia it still happens. Bush passed a law and since then it's been hard for Americans to go and exploit children. And when child prostitution is concerned, it's not done as openly in India as it is in other Asian countries, like where I've seen it in the Philippines.

Last year I was doing a crusade in the Philippines and in the resort I was shocked. I wanted to go do something about it. I saw these *old* men that came from Europe and the US sitting around with teenage girls and it was very obvious what was going on there.

CP: What was the mood among the prostitutes?

SJ: Many of them are angry. They were so loud; I've never seen women so loud. It took me about two minutes to really understand the reasons why they were so angry. Most of them, as they began to tell their stories to us, were brought there when they were very, very young. At eight or nine years old they were sold. They were told that they would have a better life in the city, they were brought from villages, they were brought from other countries, they were brought from Bangladesh which is a neighboring country, they were brought from Nepal, which is up in the north. Most of the prostitutes in India are actually brought from Nepal, which is a very poor country. And so they are told, if you go to India there will be jobs for you. And these girls were all sold when they were young and then these guys come and then they give their parents some money, and the parents are thinking maybe the children are adopted or they'll have a better life. But what's going on is they come and give them to what they call the "madams" of those brothels and they're forced into this.

The brothel that we went in the women were all, most of them were old, they were at least in their late 40s or 50s and it was sad to see young children, young boys come in, and for sex. We wanted to get to know what was going on so we found out that these women were selling their bodies for three dollars. So they charge three dollars from every customer, but these women get to keep only half of it. And 50 percent of that goes to folks around the brothel and that made me really mad. The whole place was just darkness and to know that these women all have a family back somewhere, many of them have no idea where these women are, they are completely cut off from their families. A few cases they were sending money back to their families in the villages. But the family members have no idea what they've gotten into.

CP: Can you tell me about the slabs and the cages?

SJ: I think I was there around twelve or one o'clock in the afternoon and that's when there were some customers, but that's not when it's very busy. These women work all night and they wake up very late so they were just waking up when we got there. I wanted to know "what goes on here; and where this thing happened," so they showed us a place where they have sex with the customers and where these women are kept. It's almost like small cubicles, but concrete cellars almost and there were four of them like matchboxes with a huge iron gate, and they were very tiny. And the only space there was like a concrete slab with a sheet on it and it's small and there's a wall right next to it and it's just dirty, filthy with no light, no air. There are no holes, there are no fans, there's no air circulation. And it was just the darkest place I have ever witnessed. While I was there we spent a few hours talking to these women and watching what was going on. I thought, I can't imagine anyone wanting to be there or how they're even there.

CP: What would you say to those who think the women should just run away?

SJ: I realized that they cannot run away, because there are pimps there that control them and the pimps bribe the policemen. So it's a very interesting circle where politicians are involved, the pimps are involved, and the police are involved. The other thing that I witnessed while there were cases of those with HIV and full-blown AIDS. You could tell by the change in color of their skin what was going on. But the other thing that I didn't expect was some of the customers that were there. I mean, these were the most violent men in New Delhi were right there. And that's something that I understood while being there; it's like the scum of any city is right there in places like that. I mean the murderers and the rapists; I mean the worst of the worst of a city was right there in the brothel.

CP: Is anyone there in India doing anything about the situation in that brothel?

SJ: My whole team was messed up and I said, "We need to talk about it." We went to a coffee shop and we sat together, and the man that took us there was a 6-foot, 9-inch-tall basketball player who had heard that there was a young girl from his village that was sold into there. That's how he first started going there. So when he first went in there he pretended he was a customer. He took a friend of his and they were locked up in one of the cages because a first-time customer gets locked in so that they can steal their money or whatever. And these women came, he said, and began to sit on his lap. He said, "Take all the money we have; we're not here for that [sex]." He came to look for this particular girl, but God really broke his heart that day and he's been going back ever since then. When these prostitutes fear that their children might be sold or moved from one place to another, they call this guy up and he goes and picks up their kids. Sometimes he rescues them in the middle of the night. So he has a secular job. His ministry, no funding, nothing, and his heart is to rescue these women and their children. And he began to tell us how these women are just begging him to find a way for them to get out. And the cry of these women is "Nobody cares for us. Our families don't care for us. We are getting old and our children are being sold and we want to get out of here." So we came up with a plan, right while we were there in the coffee shop. So we hired these people that have a heart and didn't have the resources, to put things in place, to start a ministry to these women.

More was shared in the interview, some of which could not be put into print. The good news is that an increasing number of people in this community are beginning to change what is happening. The bad news is that there is a long, long way to go.

PAKISTAN'S YOUNGEST SLAVES

North of India is the nation of Pakistan. Once part of the same nation, the two countries continue to have one major issue in common — modern slavery. Yet Pakistan's situation is much different from what is taking place south of its border. Rather than a growing democracy with an emerging middle class, Pakistan is more commonly known as a Taliban stronghold and one of the locations likely hosting terrorist mastermind Osama bin Laden.

But these factors do not stop Bruce Ladebu. He is a man on a mission. He's on a mission to free slaves, mainly children, toiling throughout Pakistan, through his recently formed nonprofit Children's Rescue Initiative.

UNICEF estimates that in South Asia, 44 million children are engaged in child labor. They work weaving looms, rolling cigarettes, in rope factories, and in brickfields.[2] They typically are slaves because of some debt incurred by their parents, grandparents, and sometimes great-grandparents. Due to high interest and deceit, debts only worth a few dollars in America turn into multigenerational slavery with excessive interest rates that never allow them to be paid in full.

From the time children turn five years old, they can be found at work in the brickyards where temperatures reach up to 122 degrees. After their 14- to 16-hour workday, they go into the local village to beg for food. In the process, many of the children die from disease, malnutrition, and sheer exhaustion before the time they turn 12 years old. That is, unless the child is one of the fortunate ones who come to the attention of Bruce and his team.

Over the past several years Bruce's organization has rescued a number of children who now attend school and live in freedom. I recently edited video footage provided by Bruce that was taken during a 2010 trip to Pakistan. There, he worked through local leaders to *purchase* an entire family of debt slaves from their master, a man who had forced them to work in his fields in all weather conditions, making bricks seven days a week, month after month, and year after year.

The video shows cash being exchanged and a receipt being made that declared all the family's past debts paid. The cost? In US dollars,

$285. As triumphant as the moment was for that family, Bruce was sadly philosophical in the moment. "We're going to take this family to freedom, but look at all the families we are forced to leave behind," said Bruce.

During our work together, I asked Bruce some tough questions about slavery in Pakistan and why he got involved. We also discussed tough ethical dilemmas such as buying slaves to free them. Here is part of what was shared.

CP: I know that before you entered the ministry you lived life as an adventurer, in the military, on Arctic expeditions, living among wolf populations in the Rockies, and teaching survival skills to others, to name a few. After you entered the ministry what are some the countries where you've operated?

BL: I have worked directly in Romania, Russia, Pakistan, Liberia, Kenya, Rwanda. We have members in Indonesia, Central America, all through the African countries, and so on. In 2009, after going to Pakistan, we formed the Children's Rescue Initiative, officially as an organization to start working throughout Africa and Asia to start rescuing kids from slavery, abuse, homelessness, and neglect.

CP: Tell us what kinds of slavery you see there.

BL: The kinds of slavery that we see there, in Pakistan particularly, are girls being sold into slavery of sexual nature, domestic servitude, also to labor in brick factories, little boys and girls in brick factories, rope factories, textile factories, cigarette warehouses, and I'm sure there are many more than that.

CP: Tell me about buying slaves.

BL: As we investigated, and actually went into these factories, at one of the first ones we saw a woman and a boy sitting on a bench outside a textile factory. It was a small factory. We went in to investigate and to look around and when we came out I saw that the mother was walking away and the boy wasn't there any longer. So I started asking questions. She had just sold her son into two years of labor for a $500 fee, US equivalent. I started asking questions and I found out that many, many parents will end up selling their sons because they've gotten into debt. They give their sons because of the debt or they sell the children because they need the money. So what we started doing is we started paying those debts to get the children out.

CP: Tell me about an instance where you may have been able to remove a person from a situation.

BL: The times that we take children instead of paying for them — sometimes the children are out begging because the factory owners don't give them clean water or food at all, so they have to beg. We will drive around with a team and offer the kids food, tell them we're going to take them to a safe place so we don't scare them, and then we make them disappear from the area to a place of safety. At other times we've actually gone and just taken children. One recent case was of a girl who was raped by a factory owner and became pregnant. She had three younger sisters. They were ten, eight, and seven or six [years old]. We basically, with the permission of the mayor of a big city, we took the team in and took the whole family.

CP: What are the needs? What do you need that you don't have?

BL: The biggest need, of course, is financial. It takes a lot of money to travel, to do what we do, to buy the children. Right now in one Asian country we have built an orphanage in a secret location, we have 250 children there, and we bought a house for $9,000. Half of those kids were rescued and the rest were orphans that we found.

CP: They were rescued because they would have become slaves?

BL: Yes, they were rescued because they *would have* become slaves. By the way, when girls become sexually mature they're usually shipped off to other countries as sexual slaves. They disappear. Or they are sent to houses and become personal servants and sex slaves. Our biggest needs are to continue to build orphanages and schools. We have three or four schools in Pakistan, one Christian school. In Liberia we have two Christian schools and we have one orphanage there.

There is still much work ahead for Bruce Ladebu. For every human victory the Children's Rescue Initiative celebrates they also must mourn their losses, burying children all along the way who die of malnutrition, overwork, and abuse before they can be rescued.

In an interesting turn of events, the work Bruce is furthering internationally has made an impact in the US recently as well. Just before the completion of this book, I had the opportunity to travel to Pennsylvania with Bruce along with Mark Palmer of Home of Hope-Texas. There we met with a local church group regarding the start of an aftercare center for trafficking victims in the community. Both here and to the ends of the earth, God is rising up people committed to Him and to freeing slaves to create the change that is desperately needed in our world.

BUYING AND SELLING HAITI'S CHILDREN

In 2006, I (Dillon) traveled to Haiti for the first time. My stay was at a location called Mountaintop Ministries: a school, feeding program, and church outreach in one of the most remote areas of Haiti's high mountain region. There I experienced firsthand how the efforts of everyday people from the US and Canada were saving lives from poverty, educating children, and providing spiritual assistance in areas that had rarely seen help from the outside world.

What I did not see on this first trip was anything that resembled human trafficking or slavery. That encounter took place nearly three years later when I returned in 2009. The reason I and many who travel to Haiti's countryside do not find human trafficking did not become clear until I understood the economics of the situation. The flow of buying people, particularly children, takes place from countryside to city. If you are in the country, a person might talk about having her child stay with a family member in the city or giving a child up for adoption. While this may be true, this could also account for many times when children are either given away or sold for under $100 to a *courtier* or broker who arranges deals in the city with wealthier clients.

In E. Benjamin Skinner's award-winning book *A Crime So Monstrous*,[3] he traveled undercover to negotiate his own child price. Though never following through on the deal, his investigation revealed the dark side of trafficking from an insider's perspective. Wealthy Haitians or foreigners ask around for a child to "take care of their home," performing tasks such as cleaning and laundry, then they promise housing, food, and education in return. Most of the time, these commitments are never kept.

Abuse abounds, primarily in the form of free labor, sometimes becoming sexual slavery or abusive in the process. The parents never know and simply hope life turns out better for their children.

This system seems unbelievable to most of us in a North American or European context, but consider the situation. You are a young mother of three children. There is no father, no family income, and little food to share. Night after night your children cry out for food. Malnutrition and sickness are common. With one less child to feed, the others might make it to adulthood. A businessman comes to your village and makes promises on all the right issues — money now, food, secure housing, education, and a future for your child. The deal makes sense. It will be painful, but can be rationalized by believing the child given up will be better off in his or her new place.

I've seen these looks of desperation in the eyes of Haiti's mothers. I've witnessed a brother offering to sell me his younger sister. I've watched poor, rural families give up a child to adoption with both tears of pain and hope for their child's future. I've held malnourished and mistreated children, praying God would change their plight. I've stood among family members as they mourn the death of yet another young person in their village. The pain is real. In the right circumstances, organizations can provide help to those in such situations. In the wrong circumstances, slavery takes place and the system of broken lives and a broken society continues.

Every nation is different when it comes to changing the face of slavery within its borders. In Haiti, education is key. When a child has a school to attend, is fed daily, given a school uniform, and provided learning for future opportunities, the desperate reasoning that leads to giving children into the wrong hands fades away. Haitian mothers love their children and would certainly desire to keep them at home. From my experiences in the country and in talking with others working there, the number one change that would reduce child slavery in Haiti is expanded education. When 90 percent of the schools are run by religious groups, and yet only 67 percent of primary school-aged children attend school and fewer than 2 percent graduate, it is a vast understatement to say education needs improvement.

Of course, the January 12, 2010, earthquake changed everything in Haiti. Just two weeks after the quake, which killed an estimated 300,000 people, I was standing in front of the nation's capitol building surrounded by thousands of people living in tent cities under squalid conditions. Aid was being distributed by many groups, both governmental and via NGOs, but there never seemed to be enough, especially as I traveled beyond the area nearest the airport.

On the positive side, the world responded with an amazing level of generosity following the tragedy, pumping hundreds of millions of dollars of needed money into disaster relief. In a move helpful in fighting slavery, longer-term aid has in some cases been given *only on the condition* that local communities end the *restavek* system of child bondage. If enforced, the tragedy of this devastating earthquake might have a bright side in ending slavery among tens of thousands of children. In addition, schools like the one I visited at Mission of Hope Haiti have been blessed with financial resources to literally double their school. This allows them to accommodate more than 1,000 new children by offering school twice daily, one shift in the morning and one shift in the afternoon. Progress is taking place, but only if continually monitored will the profound changes needed to eliminate child slavery in Haiti last.

And if you think Haiti's situation does not impact your community in the United States, think again. In 1999, a Haitian child was held in bondage against her will by an affluent family in Miami.[4] In the US, Europe, and in Caribbean nations, Haitians have been documented as slave laborers on farms, as domestic servants, and in the sex trade. Their problem is our problem.

It has been said all wars are ultimately civil wars because we are all brothers and sisters of one human family. What is true in war is also true in fighting slavery. When our neighbors are losing their children to slavery, should we not treat it with the same seriousness as if our own children were being taken away? How would that change how you respond to modern slavery and human trafficking? As Jesus said when talking about loving your neighbor as yourself through the story of the Good Samaritan, "Go and do likewise."

In 2009, I began sponsoring Wood Nelly Tiphia, then a six-year-old child in rural Haiti, through Compassion International. Compassion sponsors more than 64,000 children in Haiti. That is 64,000 children who will never be forced into child slavery. Wondering how to stop modern slavery worldwide? I don't have all of the answers, but Wood is one child who will not be forced into the *restavek* system, and it will be because of people who love Jesus who decided to do something.

Be the one who stands against the evil of slavery, in your community, in your country, and throughout every country of the world. In our next chapter, you'll discover some other solutions we have been discovering to help prevent slavery and rescue others from slavery in our nation and beyond.

CHAPTER 10

ARE YOU ANGRY YET?
DO SOMETHING!

C★H★A★R★L★E★S & D★I★L★L★O★N

IF YOU'RE NOT angry yet, return to page one. But if you're anything like us, you're probably ready to do something about human trafficking in our nation and possibly even in your own community.

In this chapter, we want to do two things. First, we want to be honest about the situation, meaning there is no perfect list of ten things you can do to make America slavery-free. That's our goal, but if it were that easy, somebody would have done it already (including us!). Second, we want to give you specific options you can choose to help create positive change where you live. Not many of you are ready to move to D.C. to change national policy or travel to Southeast Asia to free slaves. The good news is that you don't have to! You, along with other readers of this book, can work from where you are to help create a slave-free community, county, state, and country, with the goal of being able to say about human trafficking: "Not in my town!"

KNOW THE FACTS

As we each shared earlier in this book, the first step is to learn as much as you can about human trafficking in the United States. This book is a big jump for many of you, moving from, "I didn't know" to, "I'm ready to roll!" But please know much more research has been conducted in recent years on human trafficking. In this book's appendix, we have included a list of some of the organizations fighting human trafficking, a list of related books, and some Web sites to guide your research.

CONNECT

Our goal is to help you connect with the thousands of others in our nation interested in eliminating human trafficking in their own communities. Here are some initial steps to get connected:

- *MercyMovement.com: Our Web site provides ongoing blog updates along with a place to connect with us for further information. If something big happens in the news regarding trafficking in our country, we usually talk about it.*

- *Facebook and Twitter: If you use either of these social networks, you can look us up on Facebook.com. or Twitter.com (@ mercy_movement).*

- *Email, call, or write. Here is our contact information:*
  email: media@mercymovement.com
  Mailing address:
  The Mercy Movement
  P. O. Box 262, Franklin Springs, GA 30639
  phone: (706) 245-3143

START YOUR OWN MERCY MOVEMENT

Though we're new at this, we're already networking three venues for Mercy Movement chapters nationwide. If you are on a high school or college campus, you can start your own chapter and receive free coaching and resources to educate and equip your friends to stand against human trafficking.

If your company includes other groups supporting nonprofits, consider beginning a group to bring awareness of human trafficking to your business. Sharing information, inviting experts from the anti-trafficking movement, and supporting local causes are a huge help to fighting trafficking in your community.

And, of course, one major goal of ours is to involve local churches in fighting human trafficking. You might be the one God is calling to start the process that gets your church in the battle. Just email us and we'll give you the details.

HOST AN EVENT OR SPEAKER

We both speak across the nation on the issue of human trafficking and can be contacted through our Web site for further details. However, an event about trafficking doesn't require our presence. A local nonprofit leader, law enforcement officer, or other expert could be what you need to inform and inspire your audience to act. You can combine your efforts with other national initiatives such as the annual Stop Child Trafficking Now Walk (SCTnow.org) to raise funds to stop modern slavery.

DONATE

Every cause needs funding to operate. Fighting modern slavery is no exception. Mercy Movement raises funds for research, films and publications, advocacy, special events, and partnering with other groups to finance rescues and aftercare. You may not think you have a lot to offer, but every dollar makes a difference. You can contribute online at MercyMovement.com or contact us at the phone number or address mentioned above.

BUY FAIR-TRADE PRODUCTS

Though not mentioned in depth in this book, worldwide slavery taints many of our American-purchased products. We often do not know details, as only one part of a product is sometimes involved, but the fact remains that slavery influences our economy in a multitude of ways. To prevent such unethical labor, an entire movement known as fair trade has developed. Simply put, fair-trade products have a variety of stipulations that root out any slave labor, guaranteeing the product is 100 percent free of slave labor. We support and encourage you to support fair-trade products whenever possible in your purchases.

One organization we specifically recommend is WorldCrafts. Its mission is to bring hope to impoverished people around the world. WorldCrafts is nonprofit and a member of the Fair Trade Federation, partnering to build microenterprise businesses that provide sustainable income and hope for a better life. WorldCrafts imports handmade crafts made by artisans living on nearly every continent. To learn more about WorldCrafts, visit worldcrafts.org.

BUY SURVIVOR-MADE PRODUCTS

Increasingly, trafficking survivor groups are banding together to create jobs in the development of survivor-made goods. A favorite example of ours can be found at MadebySurvivors.com.

SUPPORT THROUGH SPORT

The Not for Sale campaign offers a unique program where your sports team can raise awareness and funding to fight slavery. Though not exclusively devoted to anti-trafficking work within the US, the concept is a great one for anyone on a team. Find out more at http://www.notforsalecampaign.org/action/athlete/.

VOLUNTEER

It's one thing to learn or even to give. It's a much deeper commitment to volunteer. Let us be clear, though. You might be angry and ready to knock down doors to start a military-style rescue operation. We do not do this! We provide education, gather evidence, and network others to eliminate the sources behind human trafficking. Law enforcement and legal teams must play the other roles in our society. That said, if you're ready to become an advocate, educator, and life-changer in this area, it's time to reach out and connect with us for ideas to get started.

PRAY

If you are a person of faith, pray every day for results to take place that reduce those suffering the abusive lifestyle of human trafficking. Whether a farm laborer in south Florida, an immigrant woman forced into the sex trade, or a domestic servant unable to leave her location, it is often prayer that paves the way for God to work. If you have the opportunity to share prayer requests with a group or church, please highlight this issue along with our efforts. We are certainly aware this is both a human and a spiritual struggle.

RESPOND

One writer in the area of human trafficking has noted that about one in three of those rescued from human trafficking in America took place have been so because an ordinary person saw something and acted. In some cases, it was noticing someone who lived a place of employment and could not leave. At other times, actions have been more direct, involving assistance to a person fleeing for help and providing a route of escape. At the very least, report suspicious activities to your local authorities as well as to the national human trafficking hotline at 1-888-3737-888, operating 24/7 in English and other languages.

SIGN A PETITION

Once, we were not very big fans of petitions, wondering if they really worked. Yet with the ease of use from modern online and mobile petitions, we are finding direct results from such efforts. A myriad of places can be found in an online search, but the best place to go is http://actioncenter. polarisproject.org/. The Polaris Project, an anti-trafficking organization in

Washington, D.C., provides direct links to the major actions taking place at the public policy or corporate level.

Specific successes we have been involved in directly or indirectly in the past year include the removal of the erotic services section at Craigslist. com, the ending of massage parlor and spa ads in *The Washington Post*, Choice Hotels' policy change regarding child prostitution,[1] and Alabama[2] and Georgia's[3] recent tightening of human trafficking laws. In fact, 2010 became a major year for increased legislation regarding human trafficking, with more than 40 new state bills enacted and more than 350 introduced nationwide.[4]

To illustrate how each person's voice matters, I (Dillon) signed a recent petition to urge California State University to make university professor Kenneth Ng shut down the sex tourism Web site he ran after the issue had been reported in a major anti-trafficking article. With *only* 298 signatures, the local newspaper soon reported the announcement that specifically mentioned the petition I had signed, which also noted the sex tourism Web site had been shut down. This is one of many examples that show how your involvement can end the abuses of trafficking in the lives of others.[5]

HOLD CORPORATIONS ACCOUNTABLE

Ever wonder what your favorite brands are doing to make sure their products are slave free? There is a great tool available to send preformatted letters to most major brands at www.chainstorereaction. com. Your two minutes might help a company choose to cut off slavery from their supply chain. As the late Neil Kearney, once president of the International Textile, Garment and Leather Workers Federation, stated, "If a business cannot afford to be ethical, then they cannot afford to be in business."[6] Free2work.org that allows users to view "ratings" of major brands by name or product type.

PREVENTION

It has been said that Benjamin Franklin coined the phrase "An ounce of prevention is worth a pound of cure." This may be even truer regarding the prevention of human trafficking. Some areas you can get involved in that could help keep future individuals from trafficking include:

- *services to runaway and homeless teenagers;*

- *refugee services;*

- *ministries and education to ethnic groups, including conversational English courses;*

- *outreach to female juvenile detention centers or prisons;*

- *your local chamber of commerce (to help stand against local businesses supporting trafficking and adult services);*

- *journalism (writing to speak out against trafficking);*

- *music and other creative arts (supporting the fight against trafficking through awareness at concerts, art galleries, and other events. As a musician, maybe you can be a version of what Natalie Grant has started at TheHomeFoundation.net.);*

- *awareness resources: wearing shirts, sporting bumper stickers, and similar merchandise to let people know about human trafficking and how they can stand against it.*

RESIST

In some of our chapters, we highlight situations where a person resisted something that supported prostitution and human trafficking in their community. For example, if you have a local publication that allows ads for spas where illegal activities have been proven or suspected, call on them to stop. Form a petition. Write a letter to the editor. Build enough tension for the publication to change what it is doing, always with respect and in a non-violent, non-threatening manner.

152 CHAPTER 10: CHARLES & DILLON

At Mercy Movement, we are continuing to investigate ways in which nonviolent protests (in the tradition of Martin Luther King Jr. and Mahatma Gandhi) can help end practices that support human trafficking. For example, if you are certain a local bank is offering an ATM machine in a location where prostitution or human trafficking is taking place, contact the bank and express your concern regarding the situation. If no action occurs, you have every right to share the information publicly and ask others to support your effort for the bank to end that practice. This is not an easy course to take, but could be what is required to see change in your area.

Some have even suggested taking a cue from the pro-life movement's practice of around-the-clock protesting in front of locations where illegal prostitution or trafficking is known to take place. For example, would anyone in your town stop at a particular spa if 50 citizens were standing in front of it with signs? Even one 24-hour period of this type of protest could attract enough local attention from media and the general public to force the business to move elsewhere. More importantly, for one day no one would be involved in the sexual services offered at this location.

I (Dillon) know this level of effort can work. The community where I live, Chattanooga, Tennessee, is currently the largest US metro area without an abortion clinic. Not one! Why? Years ago, enough people got together to protest outside of the existing clinic that it eventually left due to lack of business. Since then, any time an abortion provider has even expressed interest in a local property, committed pro-life residents band together to lease or purchase the location instead, no matter how many locations it takes, to keep the area free of abortion clinics. Despite your take on this issue, the transferrable idea is that enough people working together against locations where trafficking or similar "adult services" take place can lead to positive, long-term results.

START OR HELP WITH AN AFTERCARE FACILITY

The most recent estimate is that of the tens of thousands of sex trafficking victims in America, fewer than 50 beds are dedicated nationwide for long-term aftercare treatment. How is this even possible? While prevention and intervention are critical, there must be safe places to take those who escape and move from victims to survivors. To respond, many local and regional groups are raising funds and building their own aftercare facilities. We've connected with a few of these that will triple the number of available spaces over the next couple of years. If you feel led to do more in this area, contact our organization to talk. This is a big operation and one that requires a major financial and life investment to coordinate.

DO SOMETHING, BUT . . .

Do not attempt to investigate human trafficking in person or on the Internet as we do. Our investigators are trained professionals with many years of experience. You could easily get in over your head and find yourself injured, arrested, or even killed doing what we do.

Also, please do not attempt to do everything we have listed in this chapter. It's impossible! We can't do it all and neither can you. Having said that, reflect on the ideas listed here and *do something*. The worst thing you can do is nothing. Over time, you'll find some ideas work better than others, but you won't know unless you begin. We challenge you to consider today's victims as your own family members and to respond accordingly. Or, as Jesus said, "Go and do likewise" in showing compassion to those suffering under modern slavery.

WORTH THE EFFORT

In closing this chapter, I (Charles) want to share a few words about actually taking those first few steps to end human trafficking in your world. People often watch a film, attend a conference, or hear a speaker at school or in church who inspires or angers them about a social ill. Unfortunately, many are fired up about the issue for no more than a few days until the tension inside begins to fade. It is easy to lose our desire to act. Soon we no longer feel pain or anger and continue with life as normal, doing nothing.

Nothing.

I am asking you to remember that even when you lose your determination to "do something," that slaves will still be suffering, maybe even in or near your hometown. Don't act just on emotions. Act because if you don't act, no one else will. Act knowing that when you do respond no one may ever know your name. You might never be called a hero or a great abolitionist. Streets and buildings may not be named in your honor. There will not be a national holiday named after you. But what you do could help prevent or rescue a person for the daily agony of slavery. *Your efforts are worth it.*

I have always wanted to find the perfect words to describe how I feel when I am going undercover looking for evidence of human trafficking, organized crime, and pimp-forced prostitution. One day a friend showed me how by describing his own experiences.

My friend Clay Hearn is a missionary and humanitarian aid worker who runs an education and feeding program in a formerly war-torn region in Southern Sudan. He has survived war, tribal uprisings, poisonous snakes, land mines, mountain roads, raging rivers, and a rocket-propelled grenade explosion.

One day while we were sharing our experiences I told him of my inability to really find the right words to describe what it's like to take action instead of just reading about national or world events in the news. In our conversation, he shared the words that I'd been seeking.

He said, "Well, it's like this . . . I was moved in my heart to go to Sudan to help feed and educate children. I wanted to take action instead of sitting on the sidelines. So I sold everything I owned and made arrangements to go and work for IPHC Missions and Hope for Sudan in Kapoeta.

"When I arrived, I got out of the SUV and *there was no movie soundtrack playing.* Silence. It was just me and the sound a hot wind blowing dust so thick I tasted it in every breath I took. I looked over my shoulder, hoping God might be standing there in person to lend moral support, but I was all alone. So I unloaded my gear and got to work. Some days were boring and lonely, while others were a life-and-death fight for survival. In time, I did make a real difference that I never would have made if I had stayed at home on the couch watching the problems in Sudan unfold on network television. As for Jesus, He was there in the flesh each time I showed love and compassion to the African people, meeting physical needs for food and medical attention."

I don't make a lot of promises, but I will make two of them to your right now:

1. *If you decide to get involved in fighting human trafficking and modern-day slavery you will feel alone, ridiculed, and unsure of yourself when you first get started. You'll surely wonder where God disappeared and question whether or not you should have left the couch in the first place.*

2. *But if you stick with it, get educated about the problem in your area, and seek God through prayer for how to respond to the issues of labor and sex trafficking in your area, in time you will find you place of service and your voice in the community.*

Most of my life I have been a "man in the middle." Working undercover narcotics, operating as a bodyguard, serving as a police officer, and even in my work securing special nuclear material positioned me firmly in the middle between the people who would do you harm and your good night's sleep.

I love the middle. I *choose* it.

The middle is where the action often happens. There is no cover here and it's a place where you are completely exposed for better or for worse. In fact, the middle is usually where you will make the greatest difference! Charles J. Powell and Dillon Burroughs are in "the middle," fighting against modern slavery along with many other helpful people and organizations.

Come join us in the middle like many other others before us:

- *Mother Teresa: in "the middle" seeking to end hunger and suffering*
- *Dr. Martin Luther King Jr.: in "the middle" of the civil rights movement*
- *Mahatma Gandhi: in "the middle" seeking independence for India*
- *Jesus Christ: on "the middle" cross*

The next step is up to you. Pick an idea, go for it, and share what happens as you fight human trafficking where you are. Join the Mercy Movement!

CLOSING THOUGHTS

THE PAST TWO years have been a journey beyond our expectations. To look slavery in the eye at a personal level is deeply disturbing. To speak out and work toward change is an equally daunting task.

Our future vision includes two primary goals. First, by God's grace we are seeking to involve Christians as primary responders to modern slavery in our world, and in particular within the United States. We believe the same passion committed to past social issues within the American church can be used to push the anti-trafficking movement from *an* issue to *the* issue of our time to change. At this point, the list of prominent anti-trafficking organizations does not primarily consist of faith-based groups. Rather than adding our organization's name to the list, our dream is that five years after this book's release, when people ask who is standing against human trafficking in our world today, *Christians* are the first people to come to mind.

Second, our vision is to extend our research and partnerships beyond our current research and even beyond American borders to shine a spotlight on the issue of modern slavery worldwide. For example, time and cost restraints did not allow on-site research in Chicago, New York, Portland, Seattle, San Francisco, and other cities that serve as hot spots for trafficking and also include important organizations fighting against it. Nor did this project afford us the opportunity to investigate large-scale agricultural trafficking, an evil that exists in our local area and surrounding states, among other locations nationwide with large agricultural harvesting industries. Many are already on the front lines of this effort, including some we have mentioned in this book. If you or someone you know is involved in this way, please let us know and send them our way. Working together, our world will be changed by the compassion of Christians lived out to free slaves around the world.

Lastly, we thank you for taking the adventure with us in this book. Gathering the research used to write it has not been easy. Rather, we have each sacrificed time with family, personal finances, and even our safety at times because we firmly believe that it is all worth it to see one person escape slavery and experience the freedoms we enjoy each day. We ask for your prayers in this adventure and that you share your stories along the way as we work toward a day where every community in our nation can say regarding human trafficking, *"Not in my town!"*

ADDITIONAL RESOURCES

GROUPS AND ORGANIZATIONS

American Baptist Women (www.abwministries.org)

Anti-Slavery International: www.antislavery.org

Bal Vikas Ashram: http://www.freetheslaves.net/Page.aspx?pid=288

Campus Coalition Against Trafficking (CCAT): www.ccatcoalition.org

Center for Women Policy (www.womencenter.org) for information on
state laws

Churches Alert to Sex Trafficking across Europe (CHASTE): http://
chaste.org.uk/

Church Mission Society (CMS): www.cms-uk.org/united/index.htm

Coalition Against Trafficking in Women (CATW):
www.catwinternational.org

Coalition of Immokalee Workers (CIW): www.ciw-online.org

Coalition to Abolish Slavery and Trafficking (CAST): www.castla.org

Development and Education Program for Daughters and Communities
(DEPDC): www.depdc.org

Emancipation Network: www.madebysurvivors.com

Florida Coalition Against Human Trafficking (FCAHT):
www.stophumantrafficking.org

Free for Life Ministries, Inc.: www.freeforlifeministries.com

Free the Slaves: www.freetheslaves.net

Global Fund for Women: www.globalfundforwomen.org/

Hagar International-http://www.hagarinternational.org/

International Justice Mission (IJM): www.ijm.org

Klaas Kids Foundation (www.klaaskids.org)

La Strada International: www.lastradainternational.org

Mercy Movement: www.mercymovement.com

Nightlight Design: www.nightlightbangkok.com

Not for Sale Fund: www.notforsalecampaign.org

Polaris Project: www.polarisproject.org

Project HELP: http://www.wmu.com/projecthelp

Protection Project: www.protectionproject.org

The Redlight Children Campaign: www.redlightchildren.org

Regina Pacis Fund: http://www.arhiv.reginapacis.org/en/55.php

Restoration Ministries: www.restorationministriesdc.org

Vision Abolition: www.visionabolition.org

Vital Voices Global Partnership: www.vitalvoices.org

Rugmark: www.rugmark.org

Salvation Army: www.salvationarmy.org

Sankalp: www.sankalpindia.net/drupal

Shared Hope International (www.sharedhope.org)

Standing Against Global Exploitation Project (SAGE): www.sagesf.org

Stop the Traffik: www.stopthetraffik.org

Tiny Stars: www.tinystars.org

Woman's Missionary Union (www.wmu.org/ProjectHELP)

Woman's Missionary Union (WorldCrafts: www.worldcrafts.org

World Vision: http://www.worldvision.org/content.nsf/about/
press-child-sexual-exploitation?Open&lpos=lft_txt_Child-Sexual-
Exploitation

AFTERCARE CENTERS FOR TRAFFICKING VICTIMS

Angela's House (Atlanta, Ga.): www.juvenilejusticefund.org

Children of the Night (Los Angeles, Calif.): www.childrenofthenight.org

Courage House (Northern Calif.): www.couragetobeyou.org

Courtney's House (Washington, D.C.): www.courtneyshouse.org

Girls Educational and Mentoring Services (New York, N.Y.): www.gems-girls.org

Generate Hope (San Diego, Calif).: www.generatehope.org

Gracehaven House (Toledo, Ohio): www.gracehavenhouse.org

Home of Hope-Texas (Houston, Tex.): www.homeofhopetexas.com

Letot Center (Dallas, Tex.): http://www.dallascounty.org/department/juvenile/letotcenter.html

Mercy Ministries (Tenn. and Mo.): www.mercyministries.org

Streetlight Phoenix (Phoenix, Ariz.): www.streetlightphx.com

Traffick911 (Fort Worth, Tex.): www.traffick911.com

Wellspring Living (Atlanta, Ga.): www.wellspringliving.org

US GOVERNMENT AGENCIES ADDRESSING HUMAN TRAFFICKING:

U. S. Department of State. Yearly Trafficking in Persons Report (www.state.gov)

U. S. Department of Health and Human Services (www.acf.hhs.gov/trafficking/) Twenty-four hour hotline at the National Human Trafficking Resource Center (1.888.3737.888)

This is not an inclusive list and many other quality providers exist. This information is intended only as reference to provide opportunities for further learning and makes no claim regarding the work of individual organizations.

VIEWING & DISCUSSION GUIDE FOR DVD

THE FOLLOWING DISCUSSION guide is designed for your use as you view and share the *Not in My Town* DVD that accompanies this book. The DVD segments include an introduction followed by 8 video sessions. Each of the sessions has been produced from the research conducted by Dillon Burroughs and Charles Powell regarding human trafficking and modern slavery. The sessions focus on US cities as well as the international community. We are especially thankful to Sujo John and Bruce Ladebu for their ministry work that is also highlighted in several sessions.

TIMES:

Introduction to the Video and Discussion Guide 2:13
Session 1: Defining human trafficking 5:22
Session 2: An abolitionist's impact 13:45
Session 3: How traffickers advertise 9:14
Session 4: International trafficking 5:32
Session 5: International human exploitation 5:44
Session 6: Rescuing children and family 3:33
Session 7: Spiritual implications 5:23
Session 8: Additional Resources and credits 7:34

Search newhopedigital.com for additional content on this book, the authors, and this topic.

HOW TO USE THIS DVD

- There are a variety of ways you can use this material.

- First, you can simply watch the clips on your own and read through the discussion guide questions for your personal learning.

- However, many find it more beneficial to discuss this material with friends in a small group or class setting. We highly encourage you to find ways to use this material with others to increase awareness and action on this important topic.

- Further, the authors of *Not in My Town* are available for interviews, consulting, and speaking or seminar engagements nationwide. For more information, *see www.mercymovement.com or call (706) 245-3143.*

Thank you for taking the time to make a difference to free slaves!

DVD INTRODUCTION

This short overview helps you to gain an overview about how each of the video segments highlights chapter content and works with this viewing and discussion guide. Please note: In most of the session discussion guides, you'll find these steps repeated for your use in group sharing:

- Initiate
- Investigate
- Identify
- Intervene

For example, see how the session one steps help you to guide your group, and then proceed to use these steps with your review. Feel free to add additional questions or statements to customize the guide to your experience.

SESSION ONE

DEFINING HUMAN TRAFFICKING

INITIATE

1. According to the DVD, how is human trafficking defined?

2. How prevalent is human trafficking in today's world?

3. Does human trafficking still take place in the United States?

4. Why do you think so many people in the United States are unaware of modern slavery and human trafficking?

INVESTIGATE

5. How did Charles first become involved in investigating human trafficking? How would you feel if you had experienced the same introduction to this issue?

6. What is the goal of Mercy Movement? How does its mission move beyond mere "awareness" to action?

IDENTIFY

7. Many have unclear views regarding the Bible's teachings on slavery. However, the apostle Paul made clear in the letter of Philemon his personal intentions regarding a slave named Onesimus. Read Philemon 1:15–16 below. What did Paul wish to see happen regarding this slave who had become a believer?

> *Perhaps the reason he was separated from you for a little while was that you might have him back forever — no longer as a slave, but better than a slave, as a dear brother. He is very dear to me but even dearer to you, both as a fellow man and as a brother in the Lord.*

8. Paul's goal was not only for freedom of slaves whenever possible, but a higher calling — love. Verse 17 of Philemon says: *"So if you consider*

me a partner, welcome him as you would welcome me." Paul's request was for respect, dignity, and love toward a man who had previously been a slave to Philemon.

To claim Christianity teaches slavery or inhumane treatment of humans as acceptable is clearly contrary to the teachings of Scripture. Slavery existed in New Testament times, but Christians did not condone it. On the contrary, some of the most prominent early Christian leaders sought to free slaves whenever possible.

INTERVENE

9. First, you must personally commit to stand against human trafficking and modern slavery in all its forms. This is a natural extension of a Christian's love for God and fellow human beings. To live in apathy is to join the enemy. To fail to stand is to choose to fail. You can make an initial commitment today by signing up for more information at www.mercymovment.com.

10. In addition, many find it valuable to make a personal or group covenant to a new action. If this includes you, consider signing and dating the following statement:

"I, _____, refuse to sit and watch men, women, and children suffer the atrocity of slavery. I choose to actively work toward freeing slaves, extending services to former slave victims, and to increase consequences for those involved, directly or indirectly, the profit from the buying and selling of human beings."

Signature: _____

Date: _____

SESSION TWO

AN ABOLITIONIST'S IMPACT

INITIATE

1. Were you aware of human trafficking in Orlando? Why do you think North America's top vacation spot is also home to acts of human trafficking?

2. How is human trafficking able to "hide" within a city like Orlando?

INVESTIGATE

3. How did Charles become aware of the level of human trafficking in Orlando?

4. Who is Lynn Latham and what has she been doing to help fight human trafficking at the street level?

5. In what ways is Lynn's work successfully reaching victims in need of assistance?

6. What aspects of Lynn's work could be applied in other parts of the nation?

   In your community?

   By you?

IDENTIFY

7. In the story of the good Samaritan (Luke 10:25–37), Jesus notes that the one who stopped to help was the neighbor to the person in need. He calls us to "do likewise" and love our neighbor as ourselves. How could this apply to helping victims of human trafficking?

8. Prayer changes things. God challenges us to approach His throne of grace boldly with our requests (Hebrews 4:16). How can you help begin a movement of prayer on behalf of trafficking victims?

INTERVENE

9. Lynn's story reveals the need for personal involvement. What can you do personally to help make a difference in the fight against modern slavery? If you are in a group setting, discuss something you can do as a group. (NOTE: You can also look to the last chapter of the book for one of the ideas shared there.)

10. Talk it up: Use your Facebook status, Twitter, text messages, phone calls, or personal conversations to talk about modern slavery and what you are doing to stop it.

SESSION THREE

HOW TRAFFICKERS ADVERTISE

INITIATE

1. In what ways does human trafficking take place over the Internet? How does this form of communication make trafficking easier than before the existence of the Internet?

2. How do billboards contribute to the problem of human trafficking in America? Why are most drivers unaware of this situation?

INVESTIGATE

3. How easy is it to access victims of prostitution, including sex trafficking victims, on the Internet according to the video?

4. What are some of the ways such crimes on the Internet can be reduced or prevented?

5. How prevalent are the billboards supporting sex services in south Georgia according to the research in the video? What needs to be done to eliminate such advertising?

IDENTIFY

6. The Bible clearly teaches believers:

   Live as children of light (for the fruit of the light consists in all goodness, righteousness and truth) and find out what pleases the Lord. Have nothing to do with the fruitless deeds of darkness, but rather expose them. It is shameful even to mention what the disobedient do in secret. But everything exposed by the light becomes visible — and everything that is illuminated becomes a light (Ephesians 5:8–13).

   In what ways does this Scripture apply to Christian believers and the issues of trafficking and modern-day slavery?

   The Bible also tells us to "flee from sexual immorality" (1 Corinthians 6:18). We cannot hope to fight immorality in our culture without living with integrity in our own lives. Jesus called it removing the plank from our eye before attempting to remove the speck from another person's eye (Matthew 7:1–6).

   This is a time to get personal: What areas might need to be cleaned up in your life before working to fight trafficking over the Internet and on our nation's streets? Identify your weak spots, get help as needed, and make the commitment to represent Christ well in your own life as you seek to help make a difference in the lives of others.

7. Proverbs 31:8 teaches us to, "Speak up for those who cannot speak for themselves, for the rights of all who are destitute." In what ways does this apply to assisting victims of human trafficking?

8. In 1 Timothy 5:1–2, Paul wrote to Timothy to treat, "...younger women as sisters, with absolute purity." According to the Scriptures, men are to view younger women as their sisters. In what ways could this change how men treat women concerning the issue of human trafficking? More personally, how does this change our response to helping women caught in human trafficking? What sense of urgency is required when we view such women as our own sisters?

INTERVENE

9. Make some noise: Find an Internet marketing or billboard advertising company that allows ads supporting the sexual exploitation of women. Do something to bring attention to the issue. A letter, petition, email, phone call, letter to the editor of your paper — these are tools available to you to help others see the need for change. (NOTE: The human trafficking section at Change.org offers several current petitions that have led to numerous policy changes that oppose trafficking.)

10. Tell others: Now that you know these facts, it is up to you to share what you have learned. Take some time today or over the next few days to share this information with a pastor, organizational leader, or others who can join you in standing against human trafficking.

SESSION FOUR

INTERNATIONAL TRAFFICKING

INITIATE

1. How large is the problem of slavery in the world today?

2. Were you aware of the large number of slaves worldwide before watching or reading Not in My Town? Why do you think many are unfamiliar with the depth of this problem?

INVESTIGATE

3. What aspect about Sujo John's story impacts you the most?

4. Why do you think slavery thrives more openly in some cultures than in others? What role can we have in making a difference in problems that are so large and far away?

IDENTIFY

5. The "Great Omission" and the Great Commission: Many Christians have good intentions for reaching the world with the message of Jesus and His love. We call this the Great Commission (Matthew 28:19–20). However, western Christians are often criticized for what could be called the "Great Omission:" what we leave out in the process of missions work. In what ways does freeing slaves and showing the love of Jesus go together?

- *Trafficking victims need love and respect.*
- *Trafficking victims need physical protection.*
- *Trafficking victims are among "the least of these" and often require food, clothing, and shelter to escape their situation.*

6. What other ways do the teachings of Jesus apply to helping trafficking victims?

INTERVENE

7. Commit for the long-term: In a month, you may no longer have the same sense of urgency you do at this moment for fighting trafficking and freeing slaves. To resist this natural tendency, choose an action to help you stay alert in this effort:

- *If you are studying this material on your own, mark 30 days on a calendar, with your phone alert, in your Bible, or even on your refrigerator. Have it* serve as a reminder that, 30 days from now, you should still do something to help free slaves.

- If you are studying this material in a group, commit to reconnecting in a month, either in person or by phone, to talk about next steps to continue to stand against human trafficking.

- Let your finances follow your heart: Whatever organization you choose, find a place where you can give regularly to financially support work that frees slaves in the US and internationally. If everyone gives a little, it will do a lot in freeing many held against their will today.

- Schedule an antitrafficking event: Whether through Mercy Movement or another agency, create an event to help your community learn about modern slavery and how to stop it.

- Learn more: This book and DVD are only the beginning. Check out the other organizations and agencies in the additional resources section to continue your journey to help stop modern slavery.

SESSION FIVE

INTERNATIONAL HUMAN EXPLOITATION

INITIATE

1. How prevalent is the problem of children slaves in the world today?

2. Were you aware of the problem worldwide before watching or reading *Not in My Town*?

INVESTIGATE

3. What did you find compelling in Bruce Ladebu's interview?

4. What role can the church have in making a difference in problems that are so grave and far away?

IDENTIFY

5. In what ways does freeing enslaved children show the love of Jesus?

6. In Matthew 25:45, Jesus speaks of our work to the "least of these" as service done to Jesus Himself. A modern application of this principle is that our work to help slaves reach freedom is service given to Jesus Himself. How could this approach change how we view Christian involvement in fighting modern slavery?

INTERVENE

7. Join others: Which of the additional resources, including organizations, can help you to get involved in fighting the trafficking of children?

8. If you are already involved in some way in valuing children, share what impact you or your group is having in your community and world.

SESSION SIX

RESCUING CHILDREN AND FAMILY

INITIATE

1. What is your reaction to the methods Bruce Ladebu uses to free debt-bonded children and families? What does Ladebu explain about how his methods do not support enslavement as a way of gaining monetary benefit on the part of those who hold children and families in debt bondage?

INVESTIGATE

2. What role can the church and other groups play in this area? Do you know of examples of what your church or others are doing?

IDENTIFY

3. The church is called to live the message of Jesus. How might Jesus be working to free slaves today; He certainly is against slavery. He calls us to treat others as we would like to be treated (Luke 6:31). How would this apply to helping trafficking victims?

- *Trafficking victims are among "the least of these" and often require money, food, clothing, and shelter to escape their situation.*
4. What other ways do the teachings of Jesus apply to helping trafficking victims?

INTERVENE

5. Join others: Investigate these groups that fight trafficking. Go to the additional resources section of this book for examples. In addition, you can contact www.mercymovement.com for information on agencies in your area.

SESSION SEVEN

SPIRITUAL IMPLICATIONS

INITIATE

1. Read each of the following Scriptures:
   Luke 8:17
   Luke 4:18–19 and John 8:36
   John 1:5
   Acts 26:18
   1 John 4:18
   Psalm 146:5–10
   Psalm 74:21
   Psalm 9:9
   Psalm 118:5
   Micah 6:8 and John 8:12

INVESTIGATE AND IDENTIFY

2. How does each apply to the sessions you have viewed and the chapters you have read?

INTERVENE

3. Commit to memorize these Scriptures and to study how to take action.

SESSION EIGHT

INITIATE, IDENTIFY, AND INVESTIGATE

1. What did you learn about WorldCrafts fair trade work with FreeSet and other artisan groups that interact with those who are escaping human exploitation and trafficking?

INTERVENE

2. How will you apply this Scripture and use the resources to intervene?

Defend the cause of the weak and fatherless; maintain the rights of the poor and oppressed. Rescue the weak and needy; deliver them from the hand of the wicked" (Psalm 82:3-4).

ABOUT MERCY MOVEMENT

MISSION STATEMENT

The Mercy Movement is dedicated to seeking solutions to humanitarian crises as they occur within the United States and internationally. We seek solutions through action-oriented research and investigation, education, and nonviolent direct intervention when it is deemed necessary.

WE VALUE . . .

- Prayer . . . without it we will perish as we travel through evil places
- Seeking intelligence on human trafficking in the US and internationally
- Working with other groups who are also fighting this problem
- Rescuing slaves and helping them through recovery
- Going into a dark world far beyond the suburbs and polite conversation
- Donations from individuals, churches and corporations underwrite our efforts
- Seeking opportunities to bring attention to our cause

WE BELIEVE THAT . . .

- Those who value God, also value social justice causes
- Saving just one person from slavery is worth any financial and almost any human cost
- Presently American society is peacefully coexisting with human trafficking and slavery, mostly unaware of its presence
- Sexual exploitation in any form is a crime which claims two victims
- We cannot rely upon laws or law enforcement, politicians or governments alone to end slavery . . . individuals have a part to play.
- Human trafficking and slavery will not end until common people rise up against it their communities

ENDNOTES

CHAPTER 1

[1] David Batstone, *Not for Sale: The Return of the Global Slave Trade—and How We Can Fight It* (New York: HarperCollins, 2010), n. 2.

[2] Coalition to Abolish Slavery & Trafficking, "A Serious Problem—Around the Globe and the USA," http://www.castla.org/key-stats (accessed February 3, 2011).

[3] Christine Buckley, "From Hunter to Hunted," OC Weekly, June 28, 2007, http://www.ocweekly.com/2007-06-28/features/from-hunter-to-hunted/4/ (accessed February 3, 2011).

[4] Free the Slaves, "Slavery Today," http://www.freetheslaves.net/Page.aspx?pid=301 (accessed February 3, 2011).

[5] FBI, "Human Trafficking: An Intelligence Report," http://www.fbi.gov/news/stories/2006/june/humantrafficking_061206 (accessed February 3, 2011).

[6] Kevin Bales and Ron Soodalter, *The Slave Next Door: Human Trafficking and Slavery in America Today* (Los Angeles: University of California Press, 2009), 7.

[7] Shared Hope International, "National Report Fact Sheet," November 18, 2010, http://www.sharedhope.org/Portals/0/Documents/NationalReportFACTSHEET11.18.2010.pdf (accessed February 3, 2011).

[8] FBI, "Enforcing Civil Rights: Justice Served in the Case of the Texas Sex Slaves," http://www.fbi.gov/news/stories/2004/february/slave_021304 (accessed February 3, 2011).

[9] Free the Slaves, "Slavery Today," http://www.freetheslaves.net/Page.aspx?pid=301 (accessed February 3, 2011).

[10] Kevin Bales, "Defining and Measuring Modern Slavery," Free the Slaves, 2007, http://www.freetheslaves.net/Document.Doc?id=21 (accessed February 3, 2011).

[11] US Department of Health & Human Services, "About Human Trafficking," http://www.acf.hhs.gov/trafficking/about/index.html (accessed February 3, 2011).

[12] US Department of Health & Human Services, "Fact Sheet: Human Trafficking," http://www.acf.hhs.gov/trafficking/about/fact_human.html (accessed February 3, 2011).

[13] US Department of Health & Human Services, "About Human Trafficking," http://www.acf.hhs.gov/trafficking/about/index.html (accessed February 3, 2011).

[14] US Department of Health & Human Services, "Fact Sheet: Human Trafficking," http://www.acf.hhs.gov/trafficking/about/fact_human.html (accessed February 3, 2011).

[15] US Department of Health & Human Services, "Fact Sheet: Sex Trafficking," http://www.acf.hhs.gov/trafficking/about/fact_sex.html (accessed February 8, 2011).

[16] Ibid.

[17] Ibid.

[18] Ibid.

[19] Ibid.

[20] Ibid.

[21] Shared Hope International, Executive Summary of "The National Report on Domestic Minor Sex Trafficking: America's Prostituted Children," Shared Hope International, http://www.sharedhope.org/Portals/0/Documents/SHI_National_Report_on_DMST_2009.pdf. (accessed February 3, 2011).

[22] Jack Cloherty and Pierre Thomas, "12-Year-Old Picked Up in Child Prostitution Sweep," ABC News, November 8, 2010, http://abcnews.go.com/News/law-enforcement-child-prostitution-sweep-picks-69-children/story?id=12087740 (accessed February 3, 2011).

[23] Save Them Now, "Trafficking Questions," http://www.savethemnow.info/news/trafficking-questions (accessed February 8, 2011).

[24] IJM president Gary Haugen, interview with Glenn Beck, Glenn Beck, CNN, aired October 16, 2007, http://transcripts.cnn.com/TRANSCRIPTS/0710/16/gb.01.html (accessed February 3, 2011).

[25] US Department of Health & Human Services, "Fact Sheet: Human Trafficking," http://www.acf.hhs.gov/trafficking/about/fact_human.html (accessed February 3, 2011).

[26] US Department of Health & Human Services, "Fact Sheet: Labor Trafficking," http://www.acf.hhs.gov/trafficking/about/fact_labor.html (accessed February 3, 2011).

[27] Ibid.

[28] Polaris Project, "Types of Trafficking Cases: Types of Trafficking Cases in the United States" (Washington, D.C.: Polaris Project, 2009).

[29] "Hidden Slaves: Forced Labor in the United States," 10 (Free the Slaves and the Berkeley Human Rights Center, 2004), http://www.freetheslaves.net//Document.Doc?id=17 (accessed February 3, 2011).

[30] Ibid., 8.

[31] Polaris Project, "Human Trafficking Statistics" (Washington, D.C.: Polaris Project, 2009).

[32] Free the Slaves, "Top 10 Facts About Modern Slavery," http://www.freetheslaves.net/Document.Doc?id=34 (accessed February 3, 2011).

[33] Shared Hope International, "The National Report on Domestic Minor Sex Trafficking: America's Prostituted Children" (Shared Hope International, 2008), 8, http://www.sharedhope.org/files/SHI_National_Report_on_DMST_2009.pdf (accessed February 3, 2011).

CHAPTER 2

[1] "Testimony Before the Committee on Foreign Affairs Sub-Committee on the Western Hemisphere," US House of Representatives, submitted by Nancy Menges, Luis Fleischman, Nicole Ferrand. From The Americas Report, Center for Security Policy, March 5, 2008.

[2] MP Nunan, "Reintegrating 'restavek' children with their parents in post-earthquake Haiti," UNICEF, November 3, 2010, http://www.unicef.org/emerg/haiti_56712.html (accessed February 4, 2011).

[3] Ninette Sosa, "Child Slavery a Growing Problem in Haiti, Advocate Says," CNN Radio, July 11, 2010, http://articles.cnn.com/2010-07-11/world/haiti.child.slavery_1_restavek-jean-robert-cadet-child-slavery?_s=PM:WORLD (accessed February 4, 2011).

[4] FBI, "Human Trafficking: An Intelligence Report," http://www.fbi.gov/news/stories/2006/june/humantrafficking_061206 (accessed February 3, 2011).

[5] Kevin Bales and Ron Soodalter, *The Slave Next Door: Human Trafficking and Slavery in America Today* (Los Angeles: University of California Press, 2009), 7.

[6] Shared Hope International, "The National Report on Domestic Minor Sex Trafficking: America's Prostituted Children" (Shared Hope International, 2008), http://www.sharedhope.org/dmst/documents/NationalReportFactSheetFINAL1.7.2010.pdf (accessed February 4, 2011).

[7] See the site mentioned here at www.slaverymap.org. It is sponsored by the Not for Sale Campaign, one of the nation's leading groups in the antitrafficking movement

[8] Andy Alexander, "Post Will No Longer Accept Parlor Ads," *The Washington Post,* Ombudsman Blog, posted September 29, 2010, http://voices.washingtonpost.com/ombudsman-blog/2010/09/post_will_no_longer_accept_mas.html (accessed February 4, 2011).

CHAPTER 3

[1] Frederick Douglass, *Narrative of the Life of Frederick Douglass: an American Slave* (New Haven, Yale University Press, 1999).

[2] Dr. Martin Luther King Jr., I Have a Dream: Writings and Speeches That Changed the World (New York: HarperCollins Publishers, 1992).

[3] Official Code of Georgia Annotated, sec. 16-5-46 (a) (4) (2008).

[4] Senate Research Office, Atlanta, Georgia, "Final Report of the Commercial Sexual Exploitation of Minors Joint Study Commission."

[5] Jim Galloway, "Renee Unterman and the Fight over Child Prostitution," *The Atlanta Journal Constitution*, February 3, 2010, http://blogs.ajc.com/political-insider-jim-galloway/2010/02/03/renee-unterman-and-the-fight-over-child-prostitution/ (accessed February 4, 2011).

[6] Alexandra Priebe and Cristen Suhr, "Hidden in Plain View: The Commercial Sexual Exploitation of Girls in Atlanta," Atlanta Women's Agenda, September 2005, http://www.freedomsunday.org/downloads/Child_Prostitution.pdf (accessed February 4, 2011).

[7] Melissa Farley, Julie Bindel, and Jacqueline M. Golding, "Men Who Buy Sex with Adolescent Girls: A Scientific Research Study," The Schapiro Group, December 2009, http://www.womensfundingnetwork.org/sites/wfnet.org/files/AFNAP/TheSchapiroGroupGeorgiaDemandStudy.pdf (accessed February 4, 2011).

[8] Mickey Goodman, "Child Sexual Exploitation in Atlanta: 'You Ain't Been Down My Street,'" *Atlanta Magazine*, July 2005, http://www.mickeygoodman.com/pdf/070105-AtlMag.pdf (accessed February 4, 2011).

[9] Jim Galloway, "Renee Unterman and the Fight over Child Prostitution," *Atlanta Journal Constitution*, February 3, 2010, http://blogs.ajc.com/political-insider-jim-galloway/2010/02/03/renee-unterman-and-the-fight-over-child-prostitution/ (accessed February 4, 2011).

[10] Amy O'Neill Richard, "International Trafficking in Women to the United States: A Contemporary Manifestation of Slavery and Organized Crime," Center for the Study of Intelligence, November 1999, https://www.cia.gov/library/center-for-the-study-of-intelligence/csi-publications/books-and-monographs/trafficking.pdf (accessed February 4, 2011).

[11]William Booth, "13 Charged in Gang Importing Prostitutes," *The Washington Post*, August 21, 1999, http://www.friends-partners.org/lists/stop-traffic/1999/0363.html (accessed February 4, 2011).

CHAPTER 5

[1]M. Alexis Kennedy, PhD, and Nicole Joey Pucci, "Domestic Minor Sex Trafficking Assessment Report, Las Vegas, Nevada" (Shared Hope International, August 2007), 63, 132.

CHAPTER 6

[1]"Human Trafficking in California," report of the California Alliance to Combat Trafficking and Slavery Task Force, October 2007, 14, http://www.ohs.ca.gov/pdf/Human_Trafficking_in_CA-Final_Report-2007.pdf (accessed February 5, 2011).

[2]*Dreams Die Hard*, available for purchase from FreetheSlaves.net at http://www.freetheslaves.net/Page.aspx?pid=316 (accessed February 5, 2011).

[3]Ibid.

[4]"Man Sent to Prison for North County Sex Trafficking," San Diego 6/CW, July 26, 2010, http://www.sandiego6.com/news/local/story/Man-Sent-to-Prison-for-North-County-Sex/TdKstohEKkKrr5GMfNxfZw.cspx (accessed February 5, 2011).

[5]"Human Trafficking in California," report of the California Alliance to Combat Trafficking and Slavery Task Force, October 2007, 15, http://www.ohs.ca.gov/pdf/Human_Trafficking_in_CA-Final_Report-2007.pdf (accessed February 5, 2011).

[6]Coalition to Abolish Slavery & Trafficking, "A Serious Problem—Around the Globe and the USA," http://www.castla.org/key-stats (accessed February 3, 2011).

[7]Ibid.

[8]"Human Trafficking in California," report of the California Alliance to Combat Trafficking and Slavery Task Force, October 2007, 18, http://www.ohs.ca.gov/pdf/Human_Trafficking_in_CA-Final_Report-2007.pdf (accessed February 5, 2011).

[9]Alan Duke, "Schwarzenegger Signs California's 'Chelsea's Law,'" CNN.com, September 9, 2010, http://articles.cnn.com/2010-09-09/justice/california.chelseas.law_1_schwarzenegger-signs-parole-death-penalty?_s=PM:CRIME (accessed February 5, 2011).

[10]State of California, Assembly Bill 1844, 2010, http://www.leginfo.ca.gov/pub/09-10/bill/asm/ab_1801-1850/ab_1844_bill_20100909_chaptered.html (accessed February 5, 2011).

[11]Office of the Governor, State of California, "Gov. Schwarzenegger Signs Legislation to Combat Human Trafficking," October 11, 2009.

[12]Ibid.

[13]Bilateral Safety Corridor Coalition, overview of its history, http://www.bsccoalition.org/history.html (accessed February 5, 2011).

[14]Orange County Human Trafficking Task Force, from Task Force FAQs, http://www.egovlink.com/ochumantrafficking/faq.asp (accessed February 5, 2011).

[15]Greg Hardesty, "Domestic Prisoner Prevails," *The Orange County Register*, October 24, 2006, http://www.ocregister.com/news/shyima-44366-children-girl.html (accessed February 5, 2011).

[16] Ibid.

[17] Matt Coker, "'Slave Hunter' Co-Author Christine Buckley Wears Her Journalism on Her Sleeve," OC Weekly, July 2, 2009, http://www.ocweekly.com/2009-07-02/news/slave-hunter-co-author-christine-buckley/2/ (accessed February 5, 2011).

[18] David Batstone, Not for Sale: The Return of the Global Slave Trade—and How We Can Fight It (New York: HarperCollins, 2010), 1.

[19] Not for Sale, "About Us," account from David Batstone, http://www.notforsalecampaign.org/about/ (accessed February 5, 2011).

[20] Coalition to Abolish Slavery & Trafficking, account from "Lulu," http://www.castla.org/lulu (accessed February 5, 2011).

[21] "Church Fights Sex Trafficking in Oakland," USAToday.com, April 7, 2010, http://www.usatoday.com/news/religion/2010-04-07-oakland-trafficking_N.htm (accessed February 5, 2011).

[22] Generate Hope, grand opening press release, March 1, 2010, http://www.generatehope.org/press/press-releases/100301-GenerateHope-Program-Press-Release.pdf (accessed February 5, 2011).

CHAPTER 7

[1] Polaris Project, "Hotline Statistics" of the National Human Trafficking Resource Center, http://www.polarisproject.org/resources/hotline-statistics (accessed February 12, 2011).

[2] Texas Impact, "Texas Facts on Human Trafficking," http://texasimpact.org/UMW/HumanTraffickFactSheet.doc (accessed February 12, 2011).

[3] Amy Farrell, Jack McDevitt, and Stephanie Fahy, "Understanding and Improving Law Enforcement Responses to Human Trafficking, Final Report, 2008, June," Northeastern University, Institute on Race and Justice, 2008, http://iris.lib.neu.edu/cgi/viewcontent.cgi?article=1000&context=human_traff_res_tech_rep (accessed February 6, 2011).

[4] Ibid.

[5] Sarah Moore, "Prostitution Case Suspects Could Be Victims of Human Trafficking," Beaumont Enterprise, May 11, 2008.

[6] Ibid.

[7] Elizabeth Gibson, "Lower Swatara Crash Victims Identified," The Patriot-News, April 23, 2010, http://www.pennlive.com/midstate/index.ssf/2010/04/lower_swatara_traffic_fataliti.html (accessed February 6, 2011).

CHAPTER 8

[1] Some experts argue the same for the Canadian-US border, such as Vancouver/Seattle and Detroit/Windsor. We have yet to document statistics or specific cases on these routes.

[2] Bradley Myles, "Counting Totals of Adult Services Ads on Craigslist," Polaris Project, January 20, 2010, http://www.blog.polarisproject.org/2010/01/20/counting-totals-of-adult-services-ads-on-craigslist/ (accessed February 7, 2011).

[3] "Backpage.com to Suspend Certain Areas of Personals and Adult Sections While It Implements Solid Defenses Against Misuse," Kansas City Star, October 18, 2010.

CHAPTER 9

[1]Sujo John Ministries, http://www.sujojohn.com/story.pdf (accessed February 8, 2011).

[2]"Child Protection from Violence, Exploitation and Abuse," UNICEF, 2009, http://www.unicef.org/protection/index_childlabour.html (accessed February 12, 2011).

[3]E. Benjamin Skinner, *A Crime So Monstrous: Face-to-Face with Modern-Day Slavery* (New York: Free Press, 2008), chapter 1.

[4]Ibid., 8–9.

CHAPTER 10

[1]Amanda Kloer, "Victory! Choice Hotels Takes Action to Prevent Child Prostitution," Change.org, February 16, 2010, http://humantrafficking.change.org/blog/view/victory_choice_hotels_takes_action_to_prevent_child_prostitution (accessed February 8, 2011).

[2]State of Alabama Press Office, "Governor Riley Marks State's Success in Passage of Law Against Human Trafficking," Office of the Governor, June 25, 2010, http://www.governorpress.alabama.gov/pr/pr-2010-06-25-01-human_trafficking-photo.asp (accessed February 13, 2011).

[3]Georgia General Assembly, Senate Bill 69, 2009, http://www1.legis.ga.gov/legis/2009_10/sum/sb69.htm (accessed February 13, 2011).

[4]Michael W. Savage, "State Legislatures Step Up Efforts to Fight Human Trafficking," *The Washington Post*, July 19, 2010, http://www.washingtonpost.com/wp-dyn/content/article/2010/07/18/AR2010071801839_pf.html (accessed February 8, 2011).

[5]Change.org, "Tell Cal State Professors Shouldn't Promote Thai Sex Tourism," http://www.change.org/petitions/view/tell_cal_state_professors_shouldnt_promote_thai_sex_tourism (accessed February 8, 2011).

[6]Chain Store Reaction Web site, "Dear Consumer" section, http://www.chainstorereaction.com/dear/consumer/ (accessed February 8, 2011).

New Hope® Publishers is a division of WMU®, an international organization that challenges Christian believers to understand and be radically involved in God's mission. For more information about WMU, go to www.wmu.com. More information about New Hope books may be found at www. newhopepublishers.com. New Hope books may be purchased at your local bookstore.

Use the QR reader on your
smartphone to visit us online at
www.newhopepublishers.com

If you've been blessed by this book, we would like to hear your story. The publisher and author welcome your comments and suggestions at: newhopereader@wmu.org.

More Contemporary Issues by
New Hope Publishers

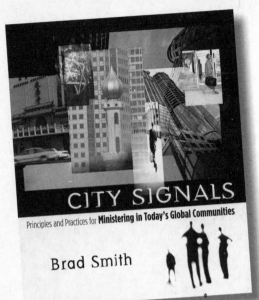

City Signals
*Principles and Practices for Ministering
in Today's Global Communities*
Brad Smith
ISBN-10: 1-59669-045-3
ISBN-13: 978-1-59669-045-5

Faces in the Crowd
*Reaching Your International Neighbor
for Christ*
Donna S. Thomas
ISBN-10: 1-59669-205-7
ISBN-13: 978-1-59669-205-3

Available in bookstores everywhere.

For information about these books or any New Hope product,
visit www.newhopepublishers.com.